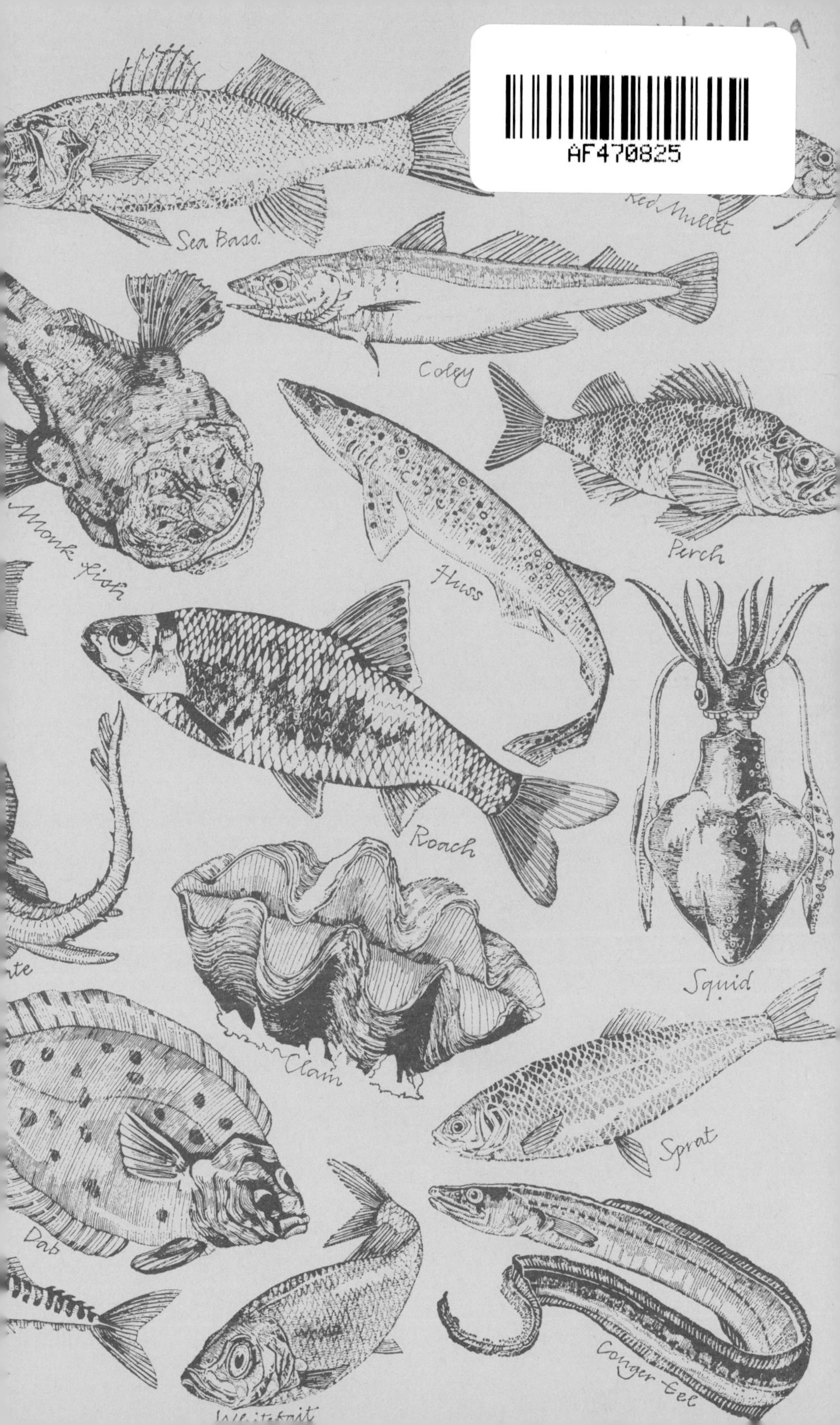

Sea Bass.
Red Mullet
Coley
Monk Fish
Huss
Perch
Roach
Squid
Clam
Dab
Sprat
Conger Eel
Whitebait

New Fish Cookery

By the same author

DEEP-FREEZE SENSE
SOUPS AND HORS D'OEUVRES
EAT WELL AND STAY SLIM
LEFT OVER FOR TOMORROW
DEEP-FREEZE COOKERY
THE BEST OF BRITISH COOKING
RECIPES FROM A COUNTRY KITCHEN

New Fish Cookery

Marika Hanbury Tenison

GRANADA
London Toronto Sydney New York

Published by Granada Publishing 1979

Granada Publishing Limited
Frogmore, St Albans, Herts AL2 2NF
and
3 Upper James Street, London W1R 4BP
866 United Nations Plaza, New York, NY 10017, USA
Q164 Queen Victoria Building, Sydney, NSW 2000, Australia
100 Skyway Avenue, Rexdale, Ontario, M9W 3A6, Canada
PO Box 84165, Greenside, 2034 Johannesburg, South Africa
CML Centre, Queen & Wyndham, Auckland 1, New Zealand

ISBN 0 246 11039 2

Printed in Great Britain by
Fletcher & Son Ltd, Norwich

Granada Publishing ®

Contents

Illustrations by Ursula Sieger

*To all those at Maidenwell who so patiently (and
only sometimes a bit impatiently) lived for so long on a
diet consisting mainly of fish in order to help test the
recipes included in the following pages. The patient guinea
pigs were Robin, Lucy and Rupert, Clare and Pancho and
all the many friends who came to lunch or dinner while
this book was being written.*

Foreword

For cooks today, whether they be a grand *chef de cuisine* or a housewife struggling to feed her family on a restricted budget, there is a whole new exciting field of food opening up and developing before their eyes – the field of 'alternative fish' – little known or overlooked breeds which have so much to offer in their own right.

Alternative fish are going to play a major part in our diets and figure significantly on our menus in the future because they are extremely valuable from a dietary point of view; cooked properly they can contribute enormously to a varied diet and, in the case of a good many of them, they are relatively inexpensive compared to the better known varieties of fish.

These 'alternative fish' are now appearing in our fish markets and on the fishmongers' slabs and the more we ask for them and buy them the greater will be their distribution and the cheaper they will inevitably become. They include huss, coley, pollock, monk fish, conger eel, the overlooked cockles and the virtually unknown mini scallops, 'queens'. There are those glorious small dabs, the underrated mackerel that is so rich and full of flavour, perch whose fillets make delicious eating, brill which rivals turbot for texture and taste and the exquisite grey mullet with its blue and silver stripes. These are just a few; the choice is wide and this book will, I hope, provide all you need to embark on a whole new range of dishes that are in step with the price problems of our times.

When I was asked to write this book I accepted immediately. What, after all, could be a better project for a cookery writer living in the west of England within thirteen miles of the north and south coasts of Cornwall and with various fish markets and harbours only a short drive away? For six months all those alternative varieties of fish filled my thoughts and, in the end, my dreams. I cooked fish, ate fish and talked fish and it could, perhaps, be a measure of the success of my dishes that my family, although they were sometimes tasting six or seven fish dishes in one day, never got bored with them. If the old maxim, impressed on me in childhood that 'if you eat fish you will grow up to be intelligent' is true, then the Hanbury Tenisons must surely be one of the most intelligent families in the country.

Obviously I picked the brains of everyone I could for new and different fish dishes. I also flipped through the pages of a hundred or more cookery books for ideas. Among those I would like to thank for the inspiration they have given me are, naturally, great cooks like Margaret Costa in her book *Food For All Seasons*, Elizabeth David for all her classics, George Lassalle and his book *The Adventurous Fish Cook* and, of course, Jane Grigson who wrote that marvellous book *Fish Cookery*. I would also like to thank the White Fish Authority for their help.

Inventing new recipes is always an excitement and with fish the scope is almost dazzling in the choice it offers. Sometimes, inevitably, I had failures or disappointments but, on the whole, both the classic and the new dishes proved easy to make and were heartily enjoyed by those who tasted them. Cooking fish brings to the housewife the chance to experiment and to produce a delicious dish in record time. She also has the pleasure of knowing that what she is producing is of real value to her family's health, at a fraction of the cost of a meat or poultry meal.

Marika Hanbury Tenison

Maidenwell　　　　　　　　　　　　　　　　　*Bel Horizonte*
Cornwall　　　　　　　　　　　　　　　　　　*Bermuda*

Alternative fish

Did you know that coley and saithe are the same fish?

Did you know that you can substitute fillets of dabs or megrim sole for dishes that use sole?

Did you know that monk fish is often used in the place of scampi because its flavour and texture are very similar to that of shrimp and lobster?

Did you know that the John Dory has a texture and flavour almost as superior as that of the considerably more expensive turbot?

Did you know that inexpensive queens taste and look like miniature scallops?

Did you know that pollock is a member of the cod family and can be used in the place of cod for a vast variety of dishes?

Did you know that mackerel is one of the most versatile fish on the market and that it is now being sold both smoked and frozen in fillets?

What are the 'alternative' fish

Considering the number of cookery books published each year, and the vast fishing waters that surround our islands, there are surprisingly few books written about fish. Those that have been published, and the fish sections in general cookery books, cover only a small percentage of the fish available in Great Britain, and concentrate mainly on the more expensive varieties such as salmon, lobster, turbot, sole, plaice, etc. They also include fish that *were* good value for money, such as herrings and cod; but these fish, sadly, have now become almost as expensive as turbot used to be and cannot really be considered fare for everyday eating.

Alternative fish are the new fish of today. The fish the housewife doesn't know enough about. They are fish that are becoming more widely available than in the past; new varieties being fished from deeper waters; and fish like mackerel which have always been around but were ignored because they did not travel well, a problem that new freezing methods have overcome. All these fish deserve to be given wider publicity, because eating them makes sense. Some are almost ridiculously cheap; others cost more but still compare very favourably with meat or poultry and have a low wastage factor combined with a very high level of protein.

The advantages of eating fish

Fish is a great budget stretcher. Even if you buy the more expensive kinds you will find there is little wastage, and even the discarded fish, bones and head can be put to good use to make delicious fish stocks which can be frozen to form the basis of a stock in which to cook other fish, or to use in soups and a vast number of exciting sauces. Unlike meat there is virtually no liquid loss or shrinkage during cooking. Cooking fish is also a help in cutting down your fuel costs; it cooks in only a fraction of the time that it would take to process the equivalent amount of meat or poultry and many of the dishes in this book take an almost remarkably short time to prepare and cook. Much of the fish you buy in the fishmonger's is already prepared and needs no preparation at all before cooking.

From the diet point of view fish can certainly help to keep us all (especially children) healthy and vigorous. For those who are slimming there is an extremely wide choice of fish dishes to choose from which will keep you fit and yet help you to remove those unwanted pounds. All forms of fish are rich in protein, minerals and vitamins. The flesh of oily fish is particularly rich in vitamin D, which is vital for growing children in order to strengthen their bones and teeth and to promote regular growth. Fish cooked whole, like sprats and whitebait, provides the essential calcium that all children and mothers badly need.

From the culinary point of view fish is a dream (I should know, I have been cooking little else for the last six months). With the more highly flavoured ones you can prepare any number of exciting dishes; with the less highly flavoured you can make use of their delicious texture to provide exquisite dishes by the addition of inventive and exciting sauces.

Why has the range of fish changed?

Some time ago overfishing brought about a frightening scarcity of the more well-known varieties of fish we used to catch around our shores. Added to that we have been having problems with the demarcation of our territorial waters and have lost many former fishing fields. As a result the commonplace cod and herring have either disappeared from the fresh fish market or become almost prohibitively expensive, and our fishermen have been turning their sights towards less well-known varieties which are still plentiful.

At the same time methods of freezing fish as soon as caught, combined with more efficient transport, have resulted in it arriving in the inland towns and cities of Britain in much better shape than ever before. Wherever you are you should now be able to buy fish that looks, smells and tastes almost as fresh as the moment it was lifted from the sea.

What are the fish used in this book?

I have tried to concentrate on fish that most housewives know little about. Buying fish can be confusing. One goes into a fishmonger, and finds a wide assortment of fish reclining on the marble slabs. Some of it may not be labelled, and if it is the names are sometimes unfamiliar. Often, in despair, one chooses the one fish whose name is recognisable and ignores those that are less expensive and often highly superior in flavour and taste. The idea of this book is to tell you all about those fish.

The price of alternative fish

Nothing fluctuates so much as the price of fish. It is always affected by weather conditions and sometimes, these days, by the fish wars that go on around our coasts. The price is also affected by supply and demand and on many occasions I have seen the same variety of fish on sale in two different places with a discrepancy of over £1 per kilogram (50p per pound) in the price. One of the most important things about buying fish is to know how to make good use of those fish on sale at a reasonable and often surprisingly low price. You may decide, for instance, that you would like some coley for supper, only to find that for some obscure reason it is suddenly being priced as an 'up market' fish. So forget about coley and buy pollock, whiting or even red fish instead; most white fish are interchangeable in made-up dishes.

I refer frequently to 'white fish' and although the White Fish Authority itself now encompasses a wider field of sea fish than those originally classed as 'white fish', for the purpose of this book I am restricting the term to mean those fish which are white when cooked, and not oily fish like mackerel.

The fish used in the recipes

Bream

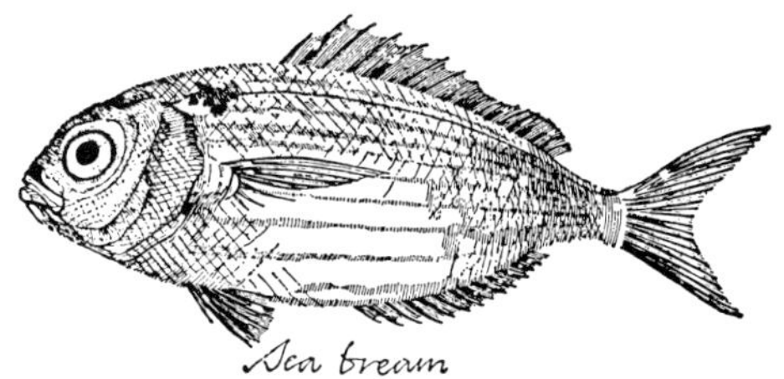

Sea bream

The sea bream, the 'porgy' in that memorable song that starts

> My Father was the keeper of the Eddystone Light
> Who slept with a mermaid one fine night,
> And of that union there came three –
> A porpoise, a porgy and the other was me . . .

is a very good fish indeed if you can find it and I am happy to say that it seems to be appearing more and more often these days.

It is an attractive oval fish, plump and pretty to look at with red fins and tail, and a large round golden eye. It should never be confused with the inferior red fish which is coarser and red all over – the body of the bream is a pretty silvery colour. The fish averages about 900 g (2 lb) in weight and the fillets can be cooked in any number of delectable ways. The whole fish can be stuffed and baked. Smaller fish can be grilled whole and served just as they are with a savoury butter, or you can poach the larger fish to serve with an exciting sauce. Use the bones from a filleted fish to make an excellent *court bouillon* or concentrated fish stock.

Brill

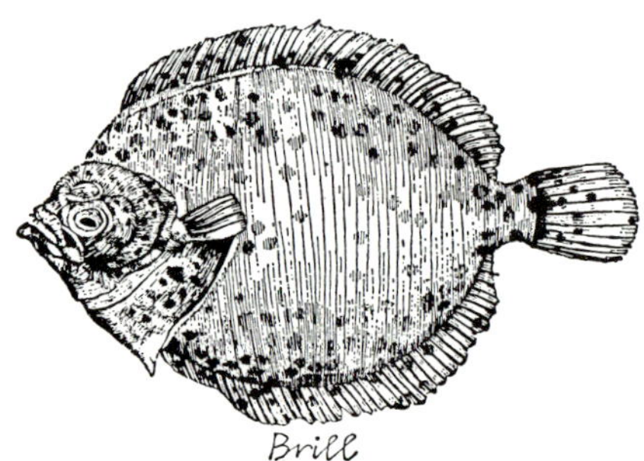
Brill

When my small son, aged seven, wants to give his approval to something he calls it 'brill' so when I buy this delectable fish (and I buy it whenever I can find it) I think about him.

Although the flavour and texture of brill is not as exquisite as that of turbot (it is the same kind of largish flat fish) it comes a very good second best and although the price is usually quite high the firm flesh and texture make it economical. It is usually sold in cutlets or steaks and I find it ideal to poach in the same way as turbot and then serve plain with a good sauce such as *Béarnaise* or *Hollandaise*. If you are poaching the fish cook it in a good *court bouillon* or in chicken stock and be careful not to overcook it. It is impossible to give accurate times for poaching fish since so much depends on its size and thickness. But if you nudge gently at the flesh around the bone with a small knife and it flakes away, then the fish is ready to be removed from the cooking liquid. If you are dealing with quite a large cut of fish and have no fish kettle with a tray in it, make a sling of foil to lay under the fish so that you can lift it up in one piece.

Brill is a perfect fish for serving cold in a salad and it is also extremely good served *au poivre* and fried in the same way as you would cook steak *au poivre*. (I use green peppercorns for this dish rather than the harsher black variety.) Crush the peppercorns (about 1 teaspoon for each steak), press them into the salted fish steaks and coat lightly with flour. Fry them quickly in butter and a little oil, then remove and add a little cream or sour cream to the juices in the pan . . . delicious!

Clams

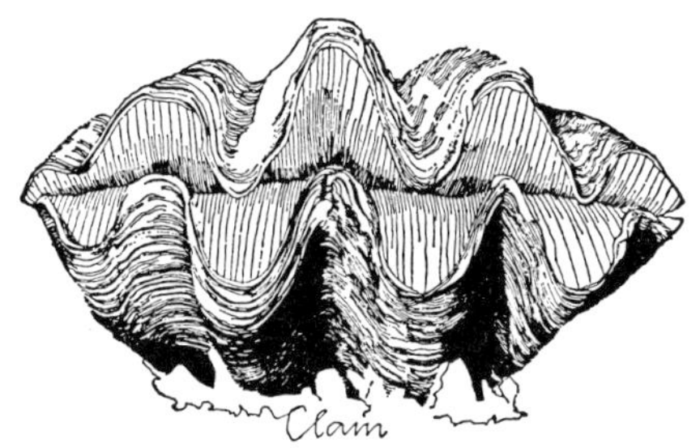

Clams are not well known in this country but they do exist. Only the other day I found soft-shelled clams (great giants) on sale for 2p each in Newton Abbot and you quite often find them on sale in London now. If you know where to go you can even dig up clams from estuaries yourself. Small clams can be eaten raw, like oysters, and I find I almost prefer their rich succulent flavour to the rather more 'iron' taste of oysters. Larger clams are too tough to eat raw and should be steamed open; then they can be stuffed and grilled in their shells, or they can be treated like scallops. Chopped clams, sold in tins, make a very good alternative to prawns in a fish cocktail.

Coley or Saithe

Saithe, also known as coley or coalfish, is now considered to be the next best thing to cod. In some ways I think it is even better, especially than frozen cod, and it is much cheaper.

When you see saithe in the fishmonger's it is not the most prepossessing of fish. It is sold filleted and has black skin and a pinky greyish tinge to the flesh. This can be off-putting, but once the fish is cooked the flesh is white, well flavoured and firm. It is an excellent fish to poach and serve with sauces, or to use in fish pies or soups, and I find it an invaluable base for fish pâtés. It is extremely good in fish cakes or home-made fish fingers. In all, it is one of the best all-rounders on sale.

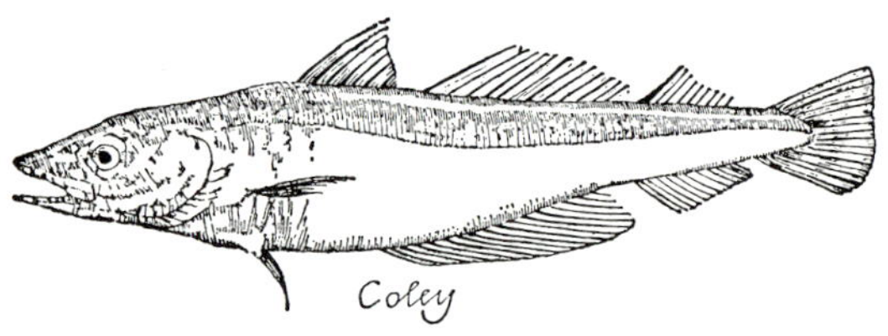

Saithe is now beginning to be smoked and looks very similar to smoked salmon. It is not cheap and I find it rather salty, but I do find it useful for garnishing and for dishes where a small amount of smoked salmon is required.

Conger Eel

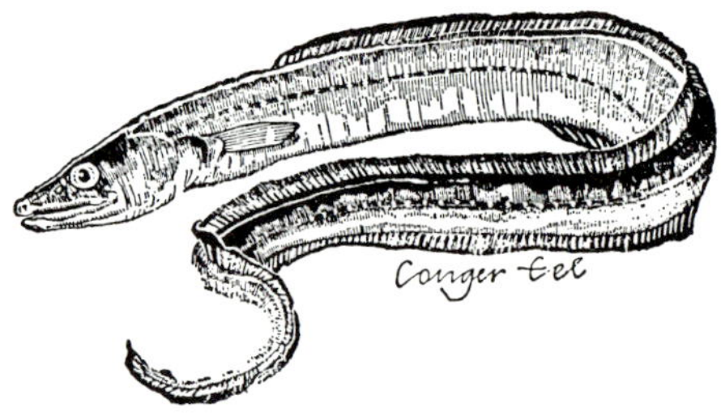

I recently began using conger as a substitute for cod in a good many dishes because it is good value, sometimes almost surprisingly cheap. Provided the flesh is not cooked too fast the meat can be tender; it is well flavoured and makes an excellent material for pies and stews.

Conger is usually sold in cutlets, but if you see a whole fish ask for a cut near the head as this will have fewer bones.

Whole steaks of conger, providing they are not too large

and coarse, can be stewed in a sauce such as tomato, and as the meat is so rich it is often a useful fish to combine with something mild like red fish in order to add flavour. The boned flesh can also be used for making kebabs and I have made very good fish cakes from the cooked flesh.

Crab

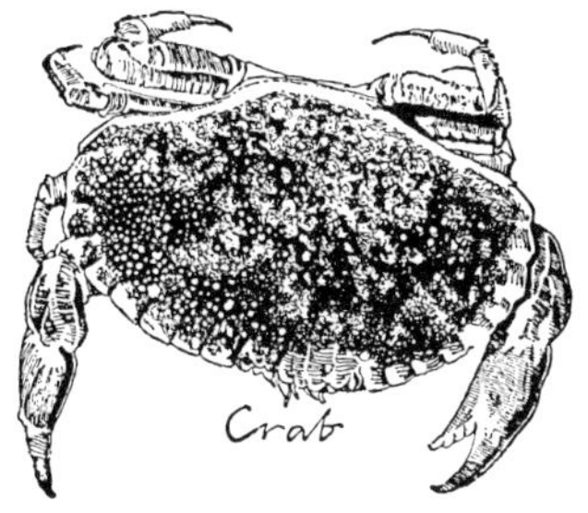

The crab is at last coming into its own as an alternative to the now ridiculously overpriced lobster. Although this shellfish is already becoming relatively expensive itself it is nevertheless still of reasonably good value since the flesh is so rich a little of it goes a long way.

Crab can be bought fresh, in the shell, either live or boiled. It is sold as a mixture of dark and white meat, with the dark and white meat sold separately or packaged and frozen. When choosing cooked crabs in the shell make sure they weigh heavily in comparison to their size to ensure they contain plenty of meat. For white meat choose a male crab (males have large, vicious looking claws) but if you prefer the brown body meat choose a female of the species who will, in the summer, have a lining of delicious pink coral. To cook a live crab, drop it into a pan of boiling salted water, boil for 3 minutes and then simmer for a further 20 minutes.

When you buy fresh crab meat that has been removed from the shell, check that it has not been stretched by the

addition of breadcrumbs or crushed rusks – this unfortunately still happens sometimes.

To dress a cooked crab, lay it on its back and twist off the
legs and claws. Push back the pointed flap curving under
the body from the shell and remove the shell. Remove the
white, feathery 'dead men's fingers' and the stomach sac
(the poisonous part of the crab which should come neatly
away in a kind of polythene bag).

Separate the meat on to two plates. Scoop out the soft,
yellow-brown meat from the shell on to one plate. Crack the
claws and legs and remove the white meat on to a second
plate. Crack the body and pick out any more white meat
from the body.

Wash the crab shell and break off the edges at the clearly
marked groove around it leaving a neat shell in which to put
your dressed crab. Brush the shell with a little oil and place
the brown meat in the centre with white meat along each
side. Serve with mayonnaise.

A crab weighing 680 g (1½ lb) should be enough for a
main course or it will provide enough crab meat for four
crab cocktails.

Crab meat can be used for any of the classic lobster
recipes. It is delicious made into croquettes, baked with a
devilled sauce or cooked with a mornay sauce.

Well worth keeping an eye open for are crab claws which
make excellent eating and which can still be bought
relatively cheaply. Always take care, when preparing crab,
that small particles of the shell do not get mixed up with
the meat.

Dabs

A popular sport in the West Country is to walk up an estuary
at low tide with a trident-shaped fork and spear in the mud
for the small flat fish known as dabs. You have to be
lightning quick and have eyes like a hawk; hence, I imagine,
the saying 'being a dab hand'.

Some maintain the dab is a muddy fish; others consider it the most highly prized member of the flounder family. I side with the latter. A really fresh dab is better by far than the rather insipid plaice, and the small, whole fish, cooked on the bone, can be almost as good as sole. The fish are usually sold at between about 200 and 250 mm (8 and 10 in)

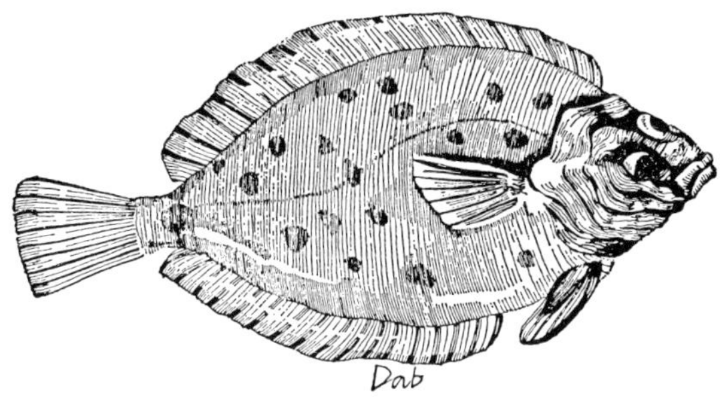

long and they can be filleted to use in any of the dishes which require a white fish or fillets of fish.

Very small fish can be egg and breadcrumbed or dipped in a light batter and deep fried whole.

Gurnard or Gurnet

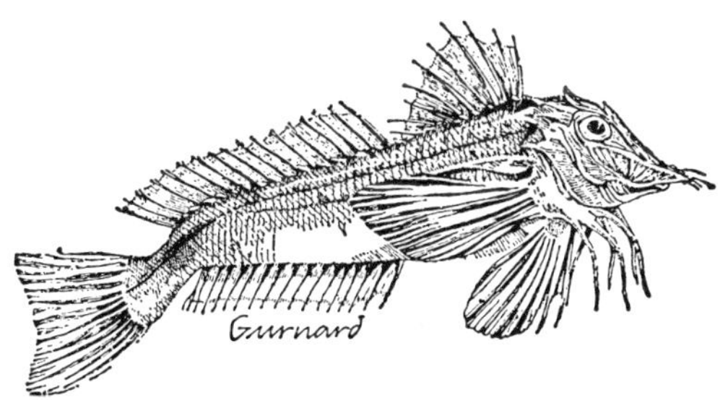

These rosy red fish are appearing more and more frequently in the fishmongers' shops and although they are often taken for mullet don't be led into believing they will have the same taste or texture. But gurnard are a good little fish in their own right, a lot cheaper than mullet, and can be used to make the most attractive dishes.

You can always tell a gurnard by the firm hammer shape of the head. Their drawback is that the heads form the major part of their bodies, and are bony. They vary from being very small (in which case they should be cooked whole) to weighing about 680 g ($1\frac{1}{2}$ lb), in which case they can be filleted and used for any of the recipes which require small fillets of fish. I usually stuff the smaller fish and bake them, while the larger ones make a useful cheap basis for fish stews and soups, with their red skins lending a pleasant colour to the dish.

Grey Mullet

Don't mix these up with the rosy-red mullet so prized along the coasts of the Mediterranean. They are not at all the same thing and don't even come from the same family. Nevertheless, their flesh is very delicious and I find them a most useful fish, especially as they are usually sold at a very reasonable price.

Grey mullet can also be confused with sea bass since they have a somewhat similar shape, but you can always tell the mullet by the pretty dark grey stripes along its body. The fish can weigh from 450 g up to about 2 kg ($1-4\frac{1}{2}$ lb), depending on the time of the year and the beds where they were caught.

I find this a most versatile fish. It can be filleted or served whole, filled with a stuffing that should include the roe if there is one (this roe, by the way, forms the true basis of taramasalata). Small whole fish are delicious grilled (especially if you can do this over a charcoal grill and if possible throw some herbs on to the fire before cooking the fish). The larger fish can be cut into chunks and then grilled. The firm flesh is good to serve cold, in salads, or it can be used for most of the made-up fish dishes which require a white fish base. The fish should be scaled before being cooked.

Most of the grey mullet caught in this country are found off the west coast and I often find them on sale in Plymouth. They are also available in London, and I think they could become a most popular fish indeed if only more people would ask for them. They travel well and are certainly a much better bet than a lot of the frozen, almost synthetic fish bought in the supermarkets. Grey mullet appear on the market during the summer and autumn months.

Huss

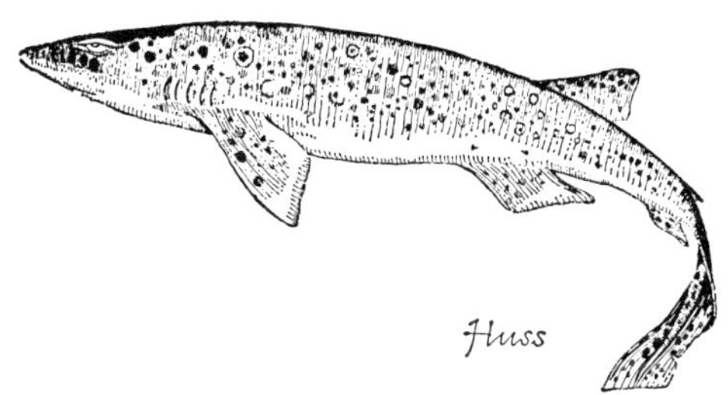

Huss may be a slightly more attractive name than 'dogfish' (one of its alternatives) but it isn't really attractive enough for this exceptionally well-flavoured and good-textured fish. I was amazed to find the tail (the only piece which appears on the market) on sale at a delightful fish stall in Lyme Regis for only 88p per kilogram (40p a pound). The proprietor, a smiling genial man with a large cheerful wife dressed as though for Ascot races, looked at me in amazement when I bought $4\frac{1}{2}$ kg (10 lb) of it. 'I know it's good,' he said, 'but are you having a fish party or something?' The answer was that I was doing exactly that. I had twenty people coming for lunch and huss was exactly what I wanted to cut into thick, finger-sized pieces to be floured, fried and served in a rich tomato sauce with boiled rice and a mixed salad.

Use huss for any dish that requires hunks of fish rather than the sort that flakes, or treat it like small eels, or fry it with any rich, robust sauce. Huss is also delicious cut into pieces, dipped in one of the batters on page 68 and deep fried until crisp.

John Dory

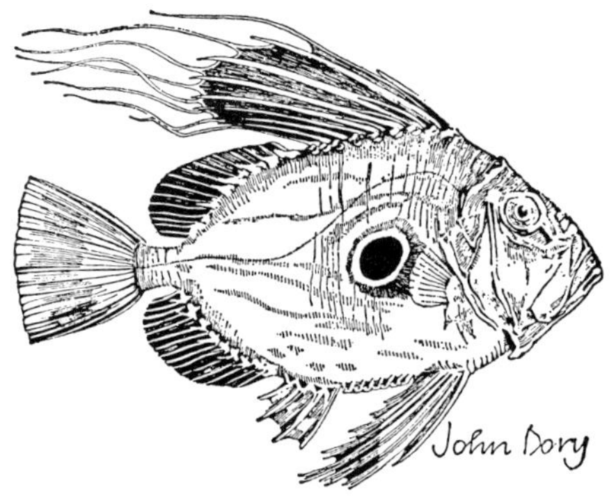

This really is one of the kings of the sea. Not the prettiest fish in the world; rather flat, with a spiny frill along its back and an ugly but appealing face. Only in England is the fish called John Dory. In most countries its name has some connotation with St Peter because it is thought that he put his thumb mark on the fish, having caught it in the sea of Galilee when Christ commanded him to cast his nets into the water; as a result the fish has a round black spot on its side.

The John Dory comes half-way between a round and a flat fish, having an oval but plumpish body. It is a difficult fish to fillet yourself so ask your fishmonger to do this job for you; larger fish of about 1.4–1.8 kg (3–4 lb) can be cooked whole and stuffed. John Dory is also one of the most perfect fish for cold fish dishes that require a firm-fleshed white fish. For these it can be cooked whole and cooled before skinning and removing the flesh from the bones.

Fillets of John Dory can be used for any recipe that requires sole, turbot or one of the more superior white fish. Buy the fish when you see it and keep asking your fishmonger to get them for you whenever he can. I have found them quite frequently during the months of writing this book and I think, if the housewife shows she is interested in them, they could become quite plentiful. They should be available most of the year.

Mackerel

I would be willing to bet that mackerel are the fish most likely to reach the top of the fish pops during the next few years. On the Continent they are already one of the most widely bought fish, and a good proportion of our catch goes across the water.

In England, except with fishermen and their families and people living right on the sea, mackerel has always been treated with some measure of disdain, formerly with good reason because this, above all other fish, has to be cooked when it is absolutely fresh. Fortunately it freezes well and if properly treated there is no reason why the fish you buy in inland cities should not taste just as good as those you used to fish out of the sea on your holidays.

So popular, indeed, is the mackerel becoming that it has already taken over from the herring as an inexpensive everyday fish. It is also a better fish, to my way of thinking, than the bony herring. The flesh has much more flavour and a far better texture and the bones are not nearly so difficult to deal with. Moreover it is far more versatile. Just look at the ways it is being sold: fillets of mackerel are frozen; the whole fish or fillets are smoked and sold as both 'hot' and 'cold' smoked fish (the hot smoked fish requires no further cooking but the cold smoked varieties need further treatment).

You can always tell whether a mackerel is fresh by a swift glance; the blue-striped skin should shine with the colours of the rainbow.

Mackerel are an oily fish and their flesh is rich. Smoked mackerel make an excellent alternative to smoked trout and are now easily available. They can be used to make excellent pâtés and pastes. Fresh mackerel form the basis of many excellent soups; they can be grilled whole or filleted; coated in oatmeal and fried like herrings; or marinated or soused and served cold.

For value for money there are very few fish that can compare with the mackerel.

Horse Mackerel

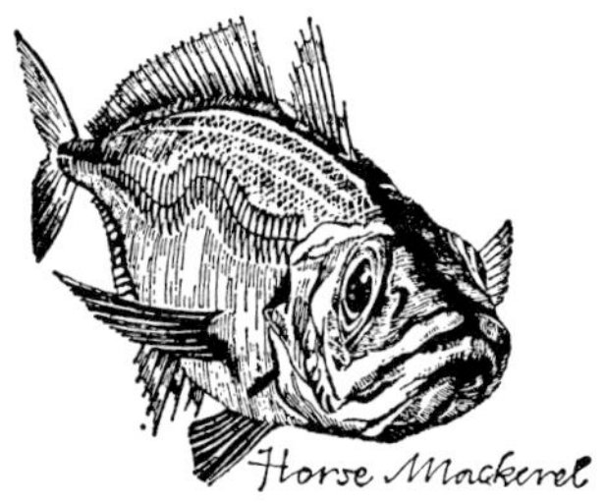

These are quite a lot larger than the usual mackerel found in our shops and their flesh is a lot more coarse. They can, however, be cheap and are perfectly all right for more basic mackerel recipes.

Megrim Sole

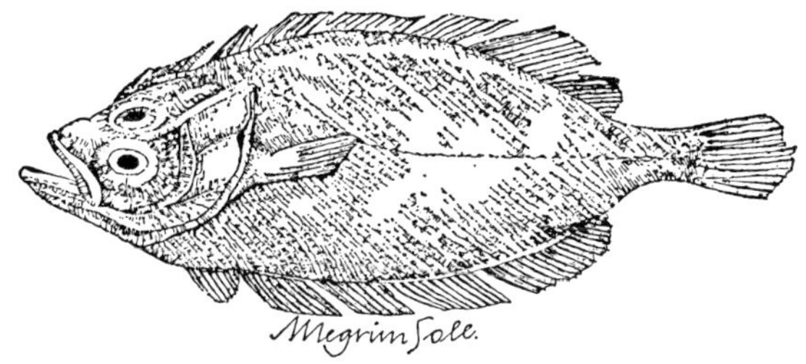

I was driving through Penzance. 'Stop,' my nose told me. 'Fish.' I parked the car practically in the middle of the street, shot up some stone steps and discovered one of the nicest and most forthcoming fishmongers I have ever met. He introduced me to the megrim sole, and I drove home far too fast because I could not wait to try it out. We had the sole grilled on the bone and it was first rate. Now I buy megrim whenever I see them and often use the fillets for some of the vast number of classic sole dishes. Although they do not make a substitute for Dover sole they are certainly as good if not better than lemon sole, and very superior to plaice, a fish I consider dreary.

The megrim is a rather long flat fish, usually weighing around 450–570 g (1–1¼ lb), and it has the rather enchanting cross-eyed look you find in most flat fish. The skin is slightly coarse and should be removed before grilling or frying.

Monk Fish

Monk fish is also known as angler fish, but it really should go under the title of 'ugly' because, if you ever see it whole, it is the kind of creature one would not like to come up against on a dark night. It is a sludgy green, with brown spots, and has the face of a tortured gnome. It weighs up to 9 kg (20 lb), with the head making up about one third of its length.

The monk fish is one of the deep sea varieties now making its mark in a big way in the fishmongers and also in restaurants where, I regret to say, it often masquerades as scampi.

Despite its looks this fish is one to buy whenever you can afford it. The flesh is superb and remarkably like that of a lobster in flavour and texture. You are in any case unlikely

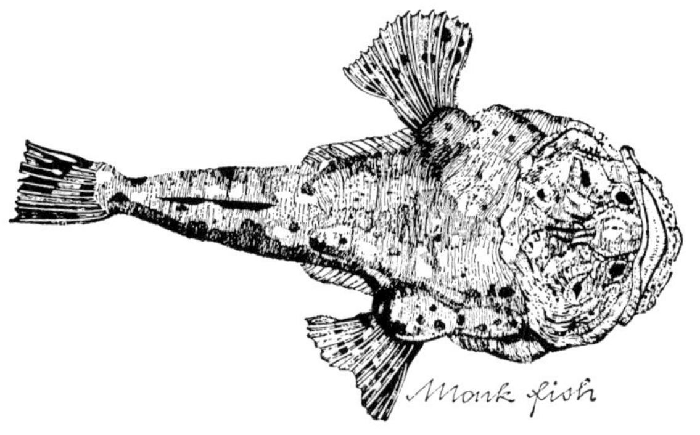

to see the whole fish, as it is usually skinned, with just the tail being offered for sale. As the flesh is so firm it makes a marvellous addition to salads and made-up dishes. You can cut it into scampi-shaped pieces and produce any number of the traditional scampi recipes, from straight fried to complicated dishes with highly spiced sauces.

Monk fish is not cheap and this, I am afraid, is mostly due to its having become so popular as a scampi substitute in restaurants. On the other hand it is a fish with little waste and with such a good, pronounced flavour and compacted texture that a little goes a long way.

Perch and Roach

Although the fish in this book are mainly from the sea I thought it worth while including the roach and the perch because I have frequently seen them in London fishmongers over the past year. The freshwater fish of this category do tend to have a slightly muddy flavour, but I find that washing them in cold water to which a little white wine vinegar has been added helps to dispel this. The fish, like most lower-echelon river fish, are a bit on the bony side, but can be filleted and in that form I find they make very good eating.

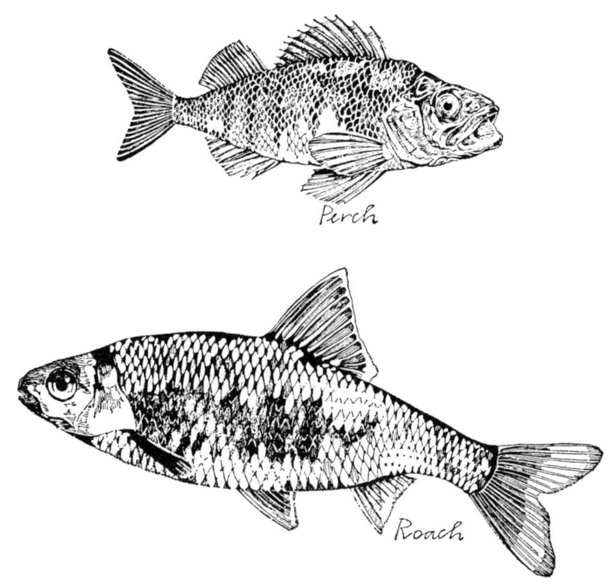

Perch and roach should be scaled as quickly as possible. If you find the scales difficult to remove with a knife, use a wire brush or dip the fish into boiling water for a few seconds to loosen them. Also remove the sharp spines along the back as soon as you start to work on the fish.

Whole small perch can be quickly fried in butter with a little oil added to it to prevent the butter burning; the larger fish can be stuffed and baked and the fillets can be grilled, fried or deep fried. Roach are rather more coarse fish and I find they are best filleted or baked in the oven.

Pollock

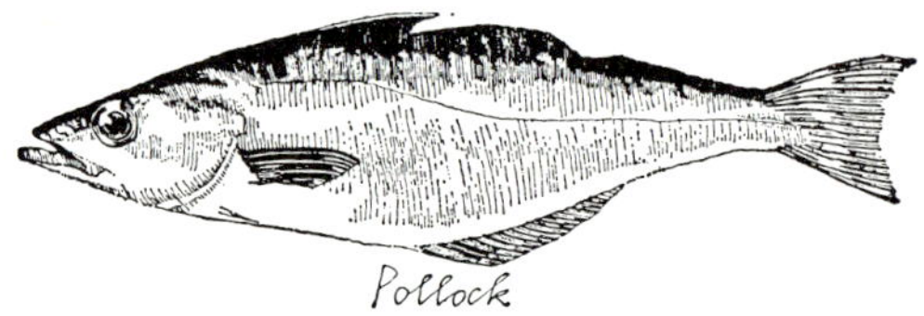

This is a fish which I first came across at my favourite restaurant, The Horn of Plenty near Tavistock. They served it cold in a sharp vinaigrette sauce with capers, and very good it was too. Afterwards, in the way these things happen, I found pollock on sale in almost every fish shop I visited, and have been buying them when I could ever since. It has a good flavour, with a finer texture than cod, and makes an excellent inexpensive basis for some very exciting fish dishes.

Pollock is a large fish, one of the cod family, and I feel it is very underrated (a good thing in a way because that helps to keep its price low). It is usually sold in cutlets or steaks and there is an extremely small amount of waste. Use it in any of the recipes which requires a firm-fleshed white fish.

Queens

If you like scallops you will certainly like queens, because they are merely a small version of the scallop, with a slightly less definite flavour but the same delicious texture. They need less preparation than scallops, are always sold cooked and can be surprisingly cheap. Queens are whiter than scallops (buy them only when they have a shine and smell fresh and sweet) and you should use them whole rather than slicing them. They are not, unfortunately, on very wide sale at the moment – most go to America, I believe to make 'clam chowder' – but there are plenty being dredged up out of the sea and they are well worth asking for whenever you get the opportunity.

Red Fish

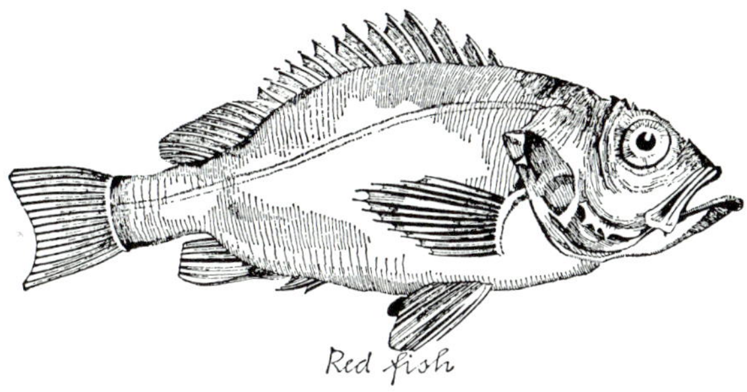

I am afraid that red fish, which are another variety that I have noticed appearing much more regularly on the fishmongers' counters, do not have the flavour one expects in such attractive looking creatures. They are a delightful bright salmon red with a sharp spiny frill along their backs. Their eyes are rather large and have a yellow gleam to them. The body of the fish is fairly substantial and they weigh up to 2.3 kg (5 lb) which makes them excellent for stuffing and baking.

Red fish should never be mistaken for the smaller red mullet which has a far superior flavour. Except for stuffing and baking, the fish doesn't really merit being served on its own but, since it is relatively cheap, it makes a good addition to soups and it is very useful indeed for made-up dishes such as fish pies, or dishes served with a strong sauce. The texture of the flesh is perfectly acceptable and, providing it is not overcooked, flakes well.

Red Mullet

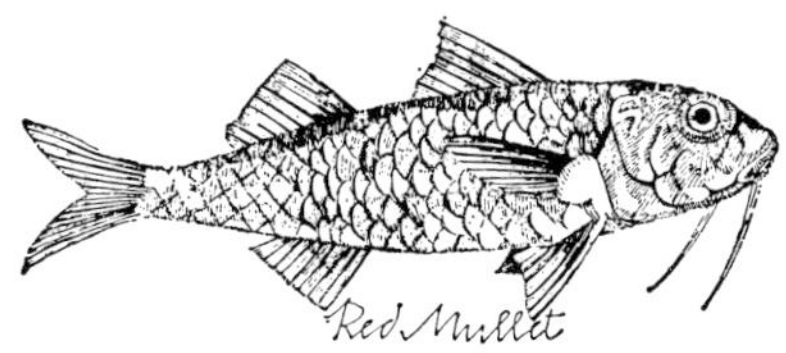

This delectable little fish, highly prized on the Continent, is not so much red as a bright rosy-sunset colour. It is easy to tell whether or not mullet are fresh because the colour begins to fade quickly and the skin becomes quite dry and hard as soon as it is past its prime. Its face is made amusing by two streamers which hang from the mouth, giving it a sage, somewhat venerable look. The scales are large and should be removed when the fish is being prepared for cooking.

Don't confuse mullet with red fish, which is similar in colour but usually a much larger fish. It is also rather plate shaped, whereas the mullet is narrow. The red fish is extremely inferior in flavour to mullet.

One of the things that sets the red mullet in a category of its own is the liver, which is not only a great delicacy in its own right but which also flavours the rest of the fish. When the mullet is cleaned the liver should always be left in place (although if you have a number of the fish it is well worth while making a small pâté from the livers in the same way as you would make a chicken liver pâté). In the smaller fish not just the liver but the whole of the insides are often left in the fish; hence its nickname 'woodcock of the sea'.

Red mullet are a fish I dearly love and it still rankles with me that, having eaten them and loved them on the Continent, I did not even know they were caught off our coasts for a long time. They have not been all that much in evidence in our fishmongers' (due to small demand) but they are fast becoming more popular and should now be appearing quite regularly on the slabs of the better shops.

Snap them up whenever you see them, and keep asking for them if you don't.

Red mullet are never large. Their usual weight is about 225 g (8 oz) and you should usually allow one fish for each serving. They tend to be on the expensive side because the demand for them in restaurants specialising in French food, and in Greek-Cypriot kebab houses, is high. But their flavour is so good they are well worth buying whenever you can.

The only possible thing that could be said against the mullet is that it is a bony fish. Larger fish, however, are no more difficult to fillet than a herring and these fillets, grilled and served cold with a marinade, are 'something else'.

Sea Bass

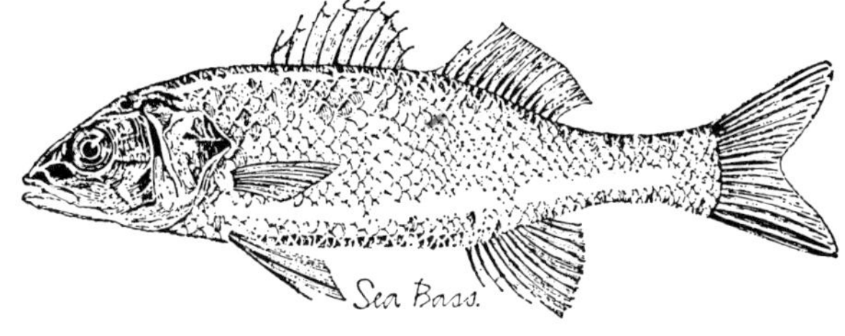

This is one of the best and most overlooked fish to be caught around our shores. The bass comes from a large family, varieties of which are found almost everywhere in the western world but the sea bass (*Morowe labrax*) is probably one of the finest varieties for taste and flavour. In France the fish goes under the name of *loup de mer* and in Italy it is called *spigola*. This is an excellent fish with an elegant line and a pleasant silvery, dark grey skin. The flesh can be rather on the soft side so the fish can be easily stuffed and baked. Steaks of sea bass are also excellent grilled or barbecued. The bass responds well to outside flavours and can be cooked in the same way as grey mullet, salmon, John Dory, etc.

Skate

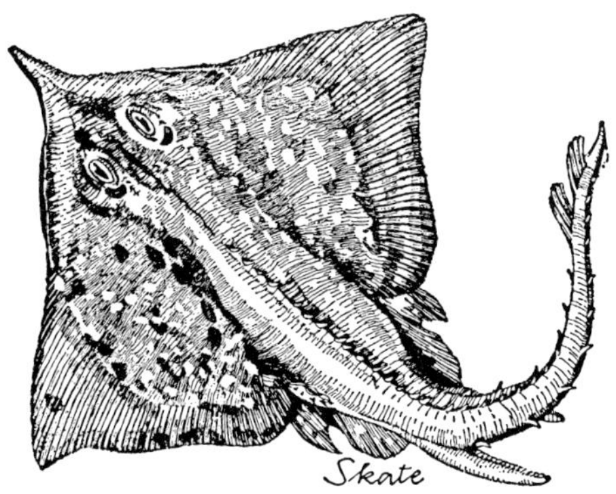

A skate straight from the sea (a form one seldom finds unless buying from a fish market or straight from a harbour) reminds me of a giant version of the rattan fans I used to buy in Malaysia when travelling there with my explorer husband. The fish has a greeny-yellow bamboo colour and spreads out flatly from a long, straight, narrow tail. The largest part of the fish are the 'wings'. The body and tail of the fish are usually thrown away and you normally see skate in fishmongers' shops as just wings or, if the fish is very large, wings cut into smaller pieces. Sometimes 'nobs' from the tails of larger fish are sold and these are very cheap indeed.

Skate wings have a lot to recommend them. Don't be put off by the slight smell of ammonia that accompanies them. This means it is good and fresh and it quickly disappears as the fish cooks. The flavour of the fish is sweet and pleasant and the texture (the flesh shreds rather than flakes) is firm and satisfying. The meat comes easily from the bones leaving the soft ribs in one piece and there are no small or sharp bones to be removed, making it an easy fish to deal with. The skin is usually removed before it is sold, but if present it can easily be stripped off once the fish is cooked.

Whole smaller wings are tender enough to be fried and the classic way of serving them is with black butter sauce.

Large wings should be poached and are delicious with an orange sauce or many of the other sauces to be found at the end of this book. You can remove the flesh from the bones and use it to make a filling for vol au vents or pancakes, but best of all I like to poach the fish, leave it to cool, shred it and use the flesh to make a cold dish or salad with mayonnaise or a vinaigrette sauce. The flesh makes an excellent alternative to tuna fish for a classic *salade Niçoise*.

Buy skate whenever you can. You can sometimes find it at bargain prices and because the bones are so easily removed it is good value for money with little wastage.

Sprats

Jane Grigson, one of the cookery writers I much admire, says that one should clean sprats through the gills. She is right, because slitting them sometimes makes them split rather like herrings (they come from the same family). On the whole though, providing you buy small rather than larger sprats, they really do not, to my mind, need to be cleaned at all. Just eat the whole thing, perhaps removing the head and tail if you feel that eating those is going too far.

In the Stockholm fish market you can see old women actually filleting sprats, with the speed of light. If you want to try this yourself (it is certainly a way to turn a very cheap fish into a four star dinner-party dish) remove the head and tail, slit the fish down the stomach, flatten it out on a board, cut side down, and then run a knife firmly over the fish, turn it over and pull the backbone out with your fingers.

It isn't as bad as it sounds and you do get better with practice. Spread the sprats with a savoury bread stuffing, roll them up, brush with a little oil, moisten with a little stock and bake for about 30 minutes.

On the whole, though, I think the best way to cook sprats is either to grill them, heads, tails, insides and all, brushing them with a little oil – they don't need much because of their natural oils – sprinkling them with salt and pepper and cooking them very close to a hot grill, turning once. The other way is to fry them without oil or fat in a very hot pan with seasoning, or to flour, salt and pepper them and then deep fry.

Like whitebait, sprats can be served as a first course, piled on a white damask napkin and accompanied with wedges of lemon and slices of buttered brown bread. The most important thing, however you cook them, is that the fish should be crisp: serve the moment they are cooked.

Squid or Cuttlefish

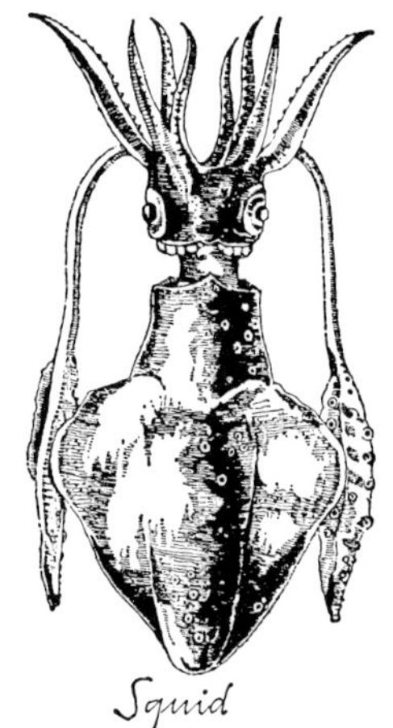

Squid

The first time I bought squid in Cornwall I was so excited to find this strange fish, which I consider to be a great delicacy, sitting in a box on the fishmonger's counter, that

I bought 1.8 kg (4 lb). 'You don't want that much, my dear,' the fishmonger told me. 'It's only good for bait and half a pound will catch you more fish than you can eat.' He was flabbergasted when I explained that I wanted to eat it.

With so many people now taking their holidays on the Continent, the traditional Englishman's reticence about something he does not know has been overcome to a great extent, and a London fishmonger I was talking to recently told me that squid, a kind of cuttlefish, are becoming more and more popular. They are, it must be admitted, a bore to clean (I have always longed to find a use for that strange plastic backbone they keep inside their sacs), but they are also inexpensive, and I find their texture one of the really great delights of fish eating. It is chewy but, providing it is properly cooked, tender at the same time; a texture you can really get your teeth into and enjoy.

Once the squid has been cleaned you can cut it into thin rings and fry the fish to serve with a tomato sauce, poach it to serve in a salad, or dip it into one of the batters on page 68 and deep fry it until the batter is crisp and the rings tender. You can also stuff the bodies of squid to make an exciting and unusual dish.

Squid, by the way, are not at all the same thing as octopus, which can be the toughest and most difficult meat in the world to digest and which needs some serious bashing and pounding to make it at all eatable. Most of the squid caught around our shores measure about 100–150 mm (4–6 in) long, and the smaller they are the more tender they will be.

To clean squid: Gently pull the heads with the tentacles on away from the body and cut off the tentacles just in front of the eye, thus removing the brain and all the other nasties. You now have the tentacles ready for cooking and you can start dealing with the bodies. On the Continent you can often buy squid ready cleaned, but in this country I am afraid you are not going to get even the most obliging of fishmongers to do the chore.

Remove the plastic-like quill and wash the inside

thoroughly to get rid of any white substance. Using a small sharp knife score through the outer, purplish skin and peel it off, leaving only the white, opaque flesh behind. Cut the flesh into thin rings. Use both the rings and the tentacles of the fish.

The Japanese are great fish cooks, probably the best in the world, and they have an excellent way of cutting large squid which makes the bodies delectably tender. Instead of slicing the bodies into rings, cut them into about 50-mm (2-in) squares. Score the squares into chequerboards, cutting only three-quarters of the way through the flesh, at about 3-mm ($\frac{1}{8}$-in) intervals. Alternatively cut the flesh into strips about 13 mm ($\frac{1}{2}$ in) wide and then cut a frill along one side, cutting right through the flesh and up to about half-way along the strips (these curl up when poached or fried and look like flowers).

Whitebait

Whitebait

Whitebait or other small fish of this size are really the ultimate in food. They don't need any preparation because there is no way in which you could possibly gut or fillet a fish of such a minuscule size. They cook in no time at all, and by eating the bones as well as the flesh you receive a high level of calcium as well as all the other protein and vitamins to be found in fish.

There is not all that much you can do with whitebait, but cooked in the traditional way, coated in seasoned flour and then deep fried, they are satisfyingly crisp. They should be drained well on kitchen paper and served as quickly as you possibly can. Left to stand they go soggy; you have probably, as I have done, eaten them in this condition in second-class restaurants.

I serve them with quarters of lemon and sprigs of deep-fried parsley. If you are being grand pile the whitebait on a white damask napkin and always accompany them with thin slices of buttered brown bread. To add an additional flavouring I season the flour which the whitebait are to be dipped into with cayenne as well as salt and pepper.

The only other way I have ever served them is marinated and well chilled. For that dish the fish are floured and fried and then covered (still warm but very well drained) with a well-flavoured and sharp vinaigrette dressing. In this form they can be served as part of a mixed *hors d'oeuvre*, or by themselves with brown bread and butter.

Whiting

These are another fish that I only really got to grips with when I began to write this book. Now I cannot get enough of them. Not only are whiting usually very good value for money but they have little wastage and their flesh is as delicate as that of a sole. The fillets can be used as a substitute for sole in hundreds of recipes and the whole fish, baked or poached, is delicious.

The poor whiting suffers from a hangover from Victorian days when they were pathetically served curled round with their tails in their mouths and, if there was an invalid in the house, you could be sure that whiting figured on their menu. At least their relative unpopularity makes them surprisingly cheap for their quality. You can split them down the back, remove the backbone and then grill them; use the flesh for fish pies, soufflés or mousses; or poach to serve with an exciting sauce.

The size of whitings on sale varies enormously. The smallest ones are usually the cheapest and these are delicious either deep fried in a batter, grilled with butter and served with lemon juice, or you can egg and breadcrumb the whole small fish and shallow fry them.

If you want to have the larger fish filleted a good fishmonger will probably do this for you, but if you do have to do it yourself you will find it quite simple once you get the knack of it.

The whiting, by way, is a member of the cod family and the flesh makes an excellent substitute for the much more expensive cod. The fish are easy to recognise: pale silvery-brown, long and slim in shape, with white bellies.

Choosing fish

The fish you buy, if it is to be worth eating, must be really fresh. This is easy to discern providing the fish is on show and not in a deep freeze cabinet. Smell, sight and touch are the three senses which play a large role in the successful choosing of fish.

SMELL

Don't be ashamed to use your nose freely in the fishmonger's shop. The smell of all fresh fish should be very 'fresh' indeed; you should be able to discern the aroma of the sea, of salt and of ozone itself. If the smell is too strong, definitely 'fishy' or somewhat ammonial, steer well away from the fish, and probably the fishmonger too.

SIGHT

Look at the fish's eyes before anything else. They must be bright and almost sparkling, clear and slightly protruding. If they are dulled over and opaque the fish will be a disappointment.

Then look at the gills. These are the red, feathery organs just behind the head on either side and they should be bright, bright red with no sign of dullness or greyness.

The scales of the fish should be bright and shining and slightly soft to the touch, the skin tight and almost glowing. If the scales are dull or the skin is dry and leathery the fish will not be fit to eat.

Shellfish should be alive or, if they have been cooked by the fishmonger, the shells should still be shining and a good, bright colour.

TOUCH

Poke at the fish with your finger if you are in any doubt as to its freshness; when it is removed the flesh should resume its shape at once. If you curl the fish up it should spring back into shape when you release it, and it should feel firm, damp and pliable. Shellfish should be heavy for their size and their tails should be springy.

CHOOSING FROZEN FISH

Check packets of frozen fish over carefully before buying them. A lot can happen between the fish being frozen and actually appearing in the commercial cabinet.

The thermometer of a commercial frozen-food cabinet should show −20 °C (−4 °F) or less. The package of fish should be rock hard and frozen solid right through. The fish should be clearly seen and not obscured by ice crystals or liquid and the package should be carefully examined to see that it is not pierced or damaged in any way.

Preparing fish

If you buy your fish from a fishmonger, especially if he is a reputable one and you are a regular customer (being on good terms with your fishmonger is just as important as with your butcher) he will almost always prepare the fish for you for the purpose for which you require it. If you buy a whole fish and ask to have it prepared he should also give you the bones and trimmings without any argument since you have already paid for these. Whenever possible do buy your fish whole and then get it prepared. The fish fillets you see on the fishmongers' slabs are often bought that way and will probably have been frozen *en route* from the sea to the shops; by buying a whole fish you can be sure that you not only get the best value for your money but also that you get the trimmings as well to make the invaluable *court bouillon* or fish stock which is needed for so many dishes.

Tell your fishmonger what you require the fish for and how you plan to serve it and then ask him if he will prepare it for you. If he won't, look around for another fishmonger; if there isn't one you'll have to learn to prepare it yourself. Cleaning and filleting fish is not in the least difficult, but like all other skills it takes a little practice; after one or two attempts you will be surprised how efficient you become.

In fairness to the fishmonger, try to shop for your fish when he is not busy, or pick out the fish you want and ask him to prepare it for you to collect later.

CLEANING

'Let this always be done with the most scrupulous nicety, for nothing can more effectually destroy the appetite, or disgrace the cook, than fish sent to the table imperfectly cleaned.' Eliza Acton.

Fortunately most fish is cleaned by the fishmonger or at source these days but there may be occasions when you have to perform the job at home so it is as well to know how to do this particular chore. Cleaning and filleting are not as difficult as they look but it is important to do the job as soon as possible after you have bought your fish. All the entrails should be wrapped in newspaper before you throw them into your dustbin; the skin and bones can be used to make the base of a nourishing fish stock.

Gut the fish before cleaning so that you will use as little water as possible in the cleaning process. Always wash the fish when you get it home, even if it has already been prepared by the fishmonger. Wash quickly under *cold* running water; do not clean in hot water or leave to soak as this will affect the flavour.

TO PREPARE WHOLE, ROUND FISH

Place the fish on a work surface with a clean damp cloth under it to prevent it slipping about. Hold firmly by the tail in your left hand and using a blunt, stubby knife or a wire brush scrape off the scales, working from the tail towards the head. Make sure all the scales are removed.

Using a sharp pointed knife, slit the fish down the length of its belly from the gills. Pull out the entrails, clean away any blood (if the blood remains stubbornly in place, rub it with some salt to help it disintegrate) and wipe the inside of the fish with a clean, damp cloth. Cut around the fins on the underside (I use kitchen scissors for this) and cut out the gills. Unless the fish is to be served whole (in which case cut out the eyes if they offend you), neatly cut off the head and tail.

TO PREPARE FLAT FISH

Using a sharp pointed knife make a cut in the cavity which lies directly behind the gills. Remove the entrails through this cut pressing the body of the fish to evacuate the guts and scraping the cavity clean with the point of the knife. Rinse the fish under fast running *cold* water and dry with a clean cloth. If the fish is to be cooked whole the head and tail should be left on; if the fish is to be filleted the head and tail should be removed. Cut the dorsal fin from the top of the back by cutting along each side and then pulling the fin firmly towards the head. Remove the fins from the underside in the same way. Wash the cleaned fish under cold water and pat really dry before proceeding with the recipe.

TO PREPARE SMALL ROUND FISH

Small fish like the larger whitebait are sometimes gutted before being cooked. This is done in the same way as gutting flat fish, through the gills. Make a small cut through the cavity behind one of the gills and press the fish gently from the tail end to evacuate the entrails. Wash well under *cold* running water.

FLOURING WHOLE FISH

If fish is to be fried it is often dredged in seasoned flour before being cooked, which results in a deliciously crisp and well-flavoured skin.

Mix your seasoning of salt and pepper in a large flat dish (a touch of cayenne gives the fish an extra lift) and press the cleaned and dried fish into the flour, making sure every bit of skin is well coated.

FILLETING FLAT FISH

Flat fish are almost always sold cleaned so this is a job that does not need to be done. Each fish will yield four fillets.

Place the fish flat on a damp cloth on a work surface top. Cut a slit on either side of the backbone as close as you possibly can to the bone and about 6 mm ($\frac{1}{4}$ in) deep on both sides. Working from head to tail, slide the knife in through the cut you have made, keeping the knife as close as possible to the backbone and sliding it from head to tail using long clean strokes and not a jabbing movement. The fillet should come cleanly away from one half of the side of the fish. Turn the fish around and cut off the second fillet, this time working from the tail to the head. Fillet the other side of the fish in the same way. Watch your fishmonger do this job a couple of times before attempting it yourself and you will see just how easy it can be; but a *sharp* knife is essential. Wash the fillets and wipe them dry.

FILLETING ROUND FISH

Place the fish on a clean damp cloth on a work surface. Clean (see page 44) and cut down the centre of its back to the bone from head to tail.

Working from the head to the tail, slide the knife with short quick strokes along the bone, keeping as close to the bone as possible. Turn the fish over and cut off the second fillet as cleanly as possible. The fillets can be cut into diagonal pieces if they are too large for your purpose.

TO SKIN FILLETS OF FLAT OR ROUND FISH

Place the fillets on a damp cloth on a work surface. Slide a sharp pointed knife along the top of the skin and below the flesh from the tail end of the fish. Hold the fish firmly by the tail and work from the tail to the head end of the fish. Use the skin as well as the bones for making a *court bouillon* or fish stock.

STUFFING FISH

Fish that is to be grilled or baked is often given a flavoured stuffing to provide extra interest to a dish. Stuff whole fish in the cleaned cavity. With fillets either sandwich two together with stuffing in between, or spread the stuffing on each fillet and then roll up neatly. With steaks remove the centre backbone and pack the stuffing into the space.

EGG AND BREADCRUMBING

Fish can also be dipped into beaten egg and then coated in breadcrumbs before being fried to give a crisp, crunchy coating.

Beat an egg with a little salt. Roll the fish in seasoned flour, dip it into beaten egg and then coat it with breadcrumbs, pressing firmly into the crumbs to make sure every bit of flesh is covered by the crumbs.

Breadcrumbs you make yourself are infinitely superior to those coloured crumbs you buy. To get fresh breadcrumbs grate stale bread through the coarse side of a grater or make the crumbs in an electric blender or food processor. To make dry breadcrumbs bake stale bread in a low oven until it is crisp throughout and a nice pale gold in colour and then crush into crumbs with a rolling pin or by putting it into a liquidiser or food processor.

OIL AND BUTTER FOR COOKING

The medium you use for cooking fish, whether it is frying or grilling, is of the utmost importance. If you use inferior products the finished dish will reflect the inferiority. This is particularly important when cooking in oil. Butters don't vary all that much in quality although, if you really want to make like a professional, I would recommend cooking with unsalted Normandy butter which, to my mind, is the best ingredient ever for cookery purposes. Salted butters are more likely to burn when they are being heated, and you should take the salting into account when seasoning.

The best oil is undoubtedly the top quality olive oil, but this, sadly, has gone beyond the means of most of us. I have been trying out various substitutes with a view to testing both quality and economy and I have finally come to the conclusion that, if you can't afford the best olive oil then the second best is sunflower oil; it doesn't have a very pronounced flavour, is pure and heats up quickly.

I still insist on olive oil when making a pure sauce such as a mayonnaise, but I use sunflower oil for other purposes.

A mixture of oil and butter is also good, as the oil prevents the butter from browning.

FREEZING FRESH FISH

There is no point in freezing any but the freshest of fresh fish at home. It will never taste any better than when you put it into the freezer and it is very liable to taste slightly worse. Remember too that when you buy fish from a fishmonger it has probably already travelled quite a considerable distance and may well have been frozen on the ship it was caught on. Try and check with your fishmonger whether the fish has already been frozen and if so don't attempt to freeze it again.

The only way you will really know if fish is 100 per cent fresh is to buy it from a fish market or from a harbour when the boats come in. If you live reasonably near the coast this is well worth doing.

Fish stock freezes well and *court bouillon* that has been used for poaching fish can be used again providing it is brought to the boil in between being thawed and re-frozen.

FREEZING WHOLE FISH

Unless you are going to use the fish fairly soon after freezing most experts say you should clean and gut it first. I find, however, that providing you do not store the fish for longer than two months and providing you take great care in wrapping it, fish preserves its flavour better if it is frozen with the guts in. If you clean and gut round fish before freezing make sure that you wash and dry it well. If it is a large fish stuff the stomach with foil to preserve the shape. If you don't gut the fish make sure that you clean and cook it as soon as the fish has thawed. If heads and tails are removed before freezing so that the fish is ready for cooking, stock should be made from them, or they should be frozen separately from the fish for use later. Cut off all sharp fins and spines before packing.

Flat fish should be gutted, washed and dried and have all fins and sharp spines removed.

Wrap fish individually (except in the case of very small fish like sprats and whitebait) in thin polythene film, then overwrap in polythene bags, seal, label and freeze.

If you plan to freeze large whole fish for any length of time it is worth taking the trouble to glaze them with a layer of ice to give them protection and prevent deterioration from air in the freezer. Open-freeze the fish, dip them in cold water, freeze again and repeat the process until the fish has a solid coating all round.

FREEZING FISH STEAKS OR FILLETS

Skin the fillets if necessary. Wrap each fillet in thin polythene film and pack them in suitable quantities in polythene bags. Steaks or fillets can also be open-frozen and then packed, but I don't find this method quite so satisfactory.

THAWING FISH

Small whole fish, fillets and steaks can be cooked from the frozen state if time is short but they will need a little extra cooking time and you may find that the outside cooks rather too fast for the centre.

Ideally all fish should be thawed in the refrigerator and used as soon as it has thawed.

ROUGH GUIDE FOR THAWING FISH IN A REFRIGERATOR

Whole fish weighing up to ... 12 hours or overnight
   1.8 kg (4 lb)
Whole fish over 1.8 kg ... 24–36 hours
   (4 lb)
Steaks and fillets ... 4–6 hours depending on size

SHELLFISH

Shellfish is tricky stuff and I don't recommend freezing it at home unless you are dealing with such items as queens or dressed crabs. In these cases prepare the shellfish for freezing and freeze it as quickly as possible. Thaw the shellfish in the refrigerator for 6–8 hours before using at once.

Commercially frozen shellfish is frozen at speeds and to depths the housewife cannot possibly hope to imitate and, providing it is well packaged, can be very good value indeed.

PRE-COOKED FISH DISHES

You can freeze any number of fish dishes, especially those where the fish is frozen in a sauce which will not separate on re-heating. Whenever possible freeze the fish in the dish in which it was cooked and re-heat immediately after thawing.

Fishcakes, breaded fish fillets, etc. can be fried straight from the frozen state but make sure they are thoroughly cooked through before serving.

Fish for diets

If you have to be on a diet, for any reason, fish can make a most important contribution to your controlled eating pattern.

Most white fish contains less than 2 per cent of fat, but is full of protein and goodness; so a poached fish dish is ideal for the dieter. They do not, however, contain as many vitamins as meat, so take care if you are on a diet to see that you get your full daily quota of vitamins to help you keep healthy while slimming.

If you are dieting seriously stick to poached or grilled fish and choose any sauces with care. There is not much point in choosing a fish dish that is not going to put any weight on you and then swamping it with a rich cream sauce.

Fish salads make very good summer dieting material and you will find a wide variety of dishes in this book that, providing you adapt them a little by cutting out the cream or other weight-adding ingredients, will help to give you a wide and varied diet.

FISH FOR INVALIDS

If you have been ill you may not feel like eating, but it's a good diet that often helps more than anything else to build up your strength and put you on your feet again. Fish dishes can be an enormous help here. They don't need long and complicated cookery processes so if you are on your own that in itself can help a lot. And fish is easy to digest, easier in fact than almost any other main ingredient. What is more, fish contains valuable proteins to help you get well again quickly.

So when you or any of your family are feeling under the

weather try some of the simpler poached fish recipes in this book. Serve small portions and keep any sauce light and simple.

Equipment for cooking fish

Don't get alarmed, you probably won't need any more equipment than you already have in your kitchen, but I thought it just worth mentioning some items which are especially useful.

A wire brush can be bought from good ironmongers and is invaluable for removing the scales from smaller fish.

A large shallow sieve is a much easier vessel in which to drain large pieces of fish than a colander. Choose one with a double thickness of mesh so that you can use it to strain stocks which need to be very pure.

Kitchen tongs and kitchen scissors are a must. The tongs are invaluable when frying fish that has to be turned without it being broken up, and kitchen scissors come in useful to clean a fish, cut off its tail, fins, etc.

Muslin may sound a rather mundane thing to have in your kitchen but I find I get through yards of it in a year. Stocks should be well purified before being used and muslin beats any sieve, however fine, for this process. It is not expensive and you can use it again and again providing you boil it between uses.

A fish kettle. If you are going to go into fish cookery in a big way then you really should invest in a fish kettle. These long, narrow pans with a perforated tray at the bottom are the only really suitable vessel in which to poach whole fish, since it can be cooked whole and then lifted out in one piece as soon as it is cooked, drained and then carefully slid on to a warm serving dish without breaking up. A fish kettle may seem a high initial expense, but a good one should last you all your life and all your daughter's life as well. I have bought two very good old-fashioned kettles in country house sales for very little and this can be a good way to save money on this kind of rather expensive equipment.

A steamer is a good buy if you don't already have one, as you can use it to steam vegetables and suet puddings as well as fish. It consists of a metal container with a perforated bottom, and a lid, designed so it will fit over different-sized saucepans.

Cooking fish

Frying

Forget memories of soggy fish and chips in newspaper because, properly done, frying can be one of the best of all ways of cooking fish. Fresh fish responds best to quick cooking and the quickest of all ways are shallow or deep frying or by grilling over or under a really high heat.

The fish should first be carefully cleaned, gutted and prepared. Dry well after washing so that the fat or oil will not spit and dust with seasoned flour or coat in egg and breadcrumbs.

SHALLOW FRYING

Most dishes that require shallow frying call for only enough fat or oil to prevent the fish from burning; usually about 6 mm ($\frac{1}{4}$ in) is sufficient. The fish should never be allowed to wallow in the fat or oil or it will become soggy and oily. Unless the fish is to be fried with other ingredients previously fried in the pan, the pan and the fat or butter inside it should be heated before the fish is added; shock from heat is part of the secret of frying.

If you are going to fry your fish in butter, one of the most delicious ways of all, then ideally the butter should be clarified before being used. This entails bringing the butter to the boil and then straining it through muslin to remove any impurities in the butter which can burn and turn brown (or worse still black) producing an unpleasant flavour. Once clarified, the butter can be kept in the refrigerator for a couple of weeks, so if you plan to fry a lot of fish it is worth clarifying a quantity of butter at a time. The butter can also be used for sealing pâtés and potted fish dishes for refrigeration.

Heat the clarified butter, oil, or oil and butter in a shallow frying pan. Heat through until really hot, add the fish and cook, unless otherwise specified, over a high heat, turning half-way through the cooking time when the bottom of the fish is golden brown. Drain the fish on kitchen paper unless it is to be served in the juices from the pan. Serve *at once* – each second it is allowed to stand around after cooking will detract from the flavour and texture. One of the things I maintain helped to ruin the fish and chip trade was that it began to be packed in greaseproof paper bags before being overwrapped in newspaper; in the old days one might have got a bit of newsprint on the chips but at least they remained crisp as the newspaper sopped up the excess grease. Now they go soggy very quickly.

Fish that respond well to shallow frying: All flat fish, whole or filleted. Mackerel, steaks or fillets of brill, coley, huss, monk fish, bass, bream, squid. Skate wings and red mullet.

DEEP FRYING

Deep-fried fish needs the protection of a floured coating, a dip in egg and then a coating in breadcrumbs, or being covered in batter; all these ingredients should be seasoned.

Deep oil is dangerous stuff. I once burnt myself badly by pouring oil which had been allowed to get *too* hot down a cold sink; the oil exploded like a volcano and I had a bandaged right arm for the whole of Christmas. Keep the hot oil well away from children, leave it to cool before straining it and never, never allow hot oil to come into contact with a cold or wet surface. Ingredients which are to be fried in deep oil should be well dried, as if damp they can easily cause the oil to rise up and overflow and then it may easily catch alight.

The oil should reach a temperature of 160–170 °C (312–325 °F). To test, drop a small piece of bread into it once a faint haze begins to rise from the surface. The bread should immediately turn a pale golden brown – if it burns the oil has been overheated. Once used the oil can be cooled, strained through muslin and used again providing it is stored in a cool place and it is only used for fish.

Prepare your fish for deep frying and keep it near the pan. Heat the oil to the correct temperature. If you are using a basket, place the fish in it (do not try to cook too many pieces of fish at the same time; they should not be touching). Carefully lower the fish into the oil and cook until the fish rises to the surface and is crisp and golden brown. Test a piece of fish to see if it is cooked through, raise the basket from the oil, leave it to drain for a few minutes and then turn out the fish on to a heated serving dish lined with kitchen paper. Keep the fish hot while frying the rest of the pieces. Remove the kitchen paper before serving and, if the occasion is a special one, serve the fish on a white napkin which will also help to absorb excess oil.

Fish that respond well to deep frying: Almost all fish can be successfully deep fried provided it is prepared in the right way. It should almost always be boned (an exception to this is mackerel which I sometimes cut into thin steaks across the bone) and the pieces of fish should not be too thick, or it will not be cooked through to the centre by the time the outside is done.

Flat fish can be cut into *goujons* (thin strips) or the fillets can be dipped in batter. Small fish such as sprats and white-bait are left whole.

Grilling and Barbecuing

Grilling is one of the best methods of dealing with fresh fish since it adds and takes away as little as possible from the intrinsic flavour. Because this method is so quick the fish must be really fresh, tender and of good quality. Do not attempt to grill larger, coarse fish.

The grill should always be pre-heated before the fish is grilled and charcoal coals should have been allowed to get red hot and then die down until grey. The fish should be oiled, marinaded or brushed with melted butter, and if it is a small fish or portion of a large whole fish, slashed through the skin to the bone at intervals to get even cooking.

It is quite impossible to be specific about cooking times – this depends on the thickness and size of the fish and the heat coming from the grill or barbecue. Just watch carefully to see when the fish is opaque and is just beginning to flake from the bone. Always serve immediately. Flat fish should be brushed with melted butter and seasoned before they are cooked, about 75 mm (3 in) from the grill or barbecue, and turned half-way through their cooking time.

Steaks of fish should be well brushed with oil or melted butter and seasoned before they are grilled. They need lubrication to prevent them drying out and should be basted with the pan juices. The fish should be placed in a well greased grill (to avoid splashing, line the pan with greased foil and place the fish on this). Thin steaks need not be turned during cooking time as the heat will be enough to cook them throughout.

Grilled fish tends to be on the dry side however well you baste it, and really should be accompanied with either a flavoured butter, placed on top as soon as it has been removed from the heat, or a sauce (see section on sauces, pages 207–244).

Fish that respond well to grilling include: Whole or fillets of flat fish, fillets or steaks of brill, red mullet, bass and mackerel.

COOKING FISH EN BROCHETTE

Many of the firm-fleshed fish, particularly monk fish, huss, grey mullet and bass respond well to being grilled *en brochette* (strung on skewers in kebab form). Fish cooked in this way can be grilled over a barbecue or under a gas or electric grill but care should be taken to see that the fish are well basted during the cooking time to prevent them drying out. The fish is sometimes marinaded before being cooked or it can be brushed with a mixture of oil and lemon juice. The pieces of fish should be large bite sized and they can be interspersed with pieces of bacon, with onion slices, bay leaves and green peppers. Cook the kebabs about 100 mm (4 in) away from the heat, turn them frequently during the cooking time and remove from the heat before the fish becomes overcooked or dries out.

Poaching

There should be no such thing as 'boiled' fish. Fish that is cooked in liquid or sauce should be 'poached' but never, never allowed to boil. If it does, the texture will be ruined and the flavour will deteriorate. Fish is a delicate substance that cannot stand rough treatment and the battering caused by fast boiling ruins it. So always poach fish gently: bring the liquid up to boiling point slowly and lower it immediately bubbles start to break the surface.

A wide variety of the dishes in this book call for the fish to be poached in one way or another and I have included under the poached fish section fish that are gently cooked in a sauce rather than being poached in the more normal way in a *court bouillon*.

A *court bouillon* (page 66) is a very important part of fish poaching. If you just cook fish in water it tends to lose flavour and become rather insipid. *Court bouillon* adds extra flavour to the fish.

A *court bouillon* is easily made from the bones, skin and trimmings (including head and tail) of fish which, providing you buy your fish from a reputable fishmonger, should always be available if you buy whole fish. If you are not able to get fish trimmings you can make a substitute *court bouillon* from a mixture of water, white wine, vegetables and herbs. If you are pushed for time and have none handy use water and a chicken stock cube. *Court bouillon* can be frozen and after use, strained and re-frozen, becoming stronger each time, providing it is brought to a fast boil in between thawing and re-freezing. To freeze *court bouillon* strain it through muslin, leave to cool and pack in rigid containers. Seal, label and freeze.

TO COOK POACHED FISH

Clean and prepare the fish for serving (some fish is cooked on the bone and then removed from the bone when cooked). Place the fish in a shallow pan. A fish kettle is invaluable because of the oblong shape, and the perforated tray at the bottom makes it easy to lift the cooked fish out of the liquid without breaking it up. If you haven't got a fish kettle make a sling out of double thickness of a foil and poke holes in it with a skewer: lay the fish on the foil, drawing up the ends to make handles.

Cover the fish with cold *court bouillon* (page 66) and bring it very gently to the boil. Lower the heat as soon as bubbles begin to break the surface and cook just below boiling point, so that the water is barely moving, until the flesh turns opaque and begins to flake from the bone. Remove the fish and drain off as much liquid as possible before continuing with the recipe.

Fish that respond well to poaching: Almost all fish, provided care is taken not to overcook it.

Steaming

I have virtually excluded steamed fish from this book because I felt that this way of cooking fish turns people's memories to the fish of their childhood, badly cooked at school, or to invalid food. In fact steaming, providing it is carefully timed, is an excellent way to cook fish, especially if it is very fresh, and if you are worried about calories. It is a quick and efficient way to cook the better quality fish, and is also good for those that have firm but large textured flesh, such as coley, John Dory, monk fish, huss, bass, grey mullet, etc.

To get the timing exact keep testing the fish by looking and feeling. Properly cooked steamed fish should be opaque, firm but resilient to the touch (a slight pressure of a finger will be enough, with practice, to tell you whether the fish is cooked) and just flaking from the bones. Remove from the heat immediately.

The best thing to cook the fish in is a steamer. Line it with buttered foil to keep in all the flavour, put in the fish, skin side down and not overcrowded, and cook over just-boiling water. If you have no steamer the fish can be put on a buttered plate and set over a saucepan of hot water that is just at boiling point and covered with the pan lid.

Fish that respond well to steaming: Almost all the fish that require poaching in *court bouillon*, providing they are fresh and of a fairly fine texture. Oily fish such as red mullet and mackerel and tougher-textured fish such as conger eel and squid are not suitable.

Baking

A large section in this book comes under this heading because 'baking fish is safe'. Any other method needs careful timing, but as when baking fish you both seal in the flavours and, usually, add extra flavours by marinading or cooking with other ingredients, a few minutes overcooking does not matter too much. Also you are using a process which does not need much supervision: in some recipes the fish needs to be basted now and then but usually it is left alone.

Fish can be wrapped in foil and then baked, or placed in a baking dish with liquid, butter, oil or a sauce (always butter or oil the dish before cooking to prevent the fish sticking). Whatever you do, don't allow the fish to dry out; it can overcook a little but it must never be allowed to dry. I have given baking times in the recipes but do follow your own judgment rather than mine because you can see how thick the fish is and whether the flesh is getting dry and scaly.

Always check the fish during the last 10 minutes of cooking time to see whether the flesh is opaque and beginning to flake away from the bone (and when in doubt baste with the juices in the pan). If this is happening the fish is cooked and should be removed from the oven immediately.

Fish that respond well to baking: All the fish in this book.

EN PAPILLOTE

This is the term used for fish cooked in the oven in grease-proof parcels or, these days, tinfoil packages. This method of cooking allows the fish to cook in its own juices and is particularly good for fresh, tender fish with a fine texture and good flavour.

BRAISING

This is the term used for fish cooked in the oven with vegetables or a sauce. It can be used for most fish; braised fish are grouped with baked in this book.

Marinaded fish

Fish is said to be cooked when it loses the translucent quality of its flesh. This can also be achieved by marinading, a process that is particularly successful with oily fish such as mackerel, or with the best quality white fish fillets.

Many fish can be marinaded before being cooked, thereby gaining flavour and tenderness.

Some recipes require the fish to be cooked and then marinaded to serve cold.

Cold fish dishes

I feel very strongly that this is one of the most unexploited areas of fish cookery in this country. There are so many delicious fish dishes that can be served cold and they make very good starters or summer main courses. Often a chilled dish brings out the flavour of the fish even more than a hot one can, and these dishes always look attractive and appetising.

Like all cold food, cold fish dishes should be carefully served and well garnished. Care should be taken with their colour as well as their general appearance.

For example, arranging the fish on a bed of crisp lettuce leaves provides a contrast of colour, flavour and texture. Use your imagination and garnish dishes with finely chopped parsley, chervil or chives, slices or wedges of lemon, thin strips of tinned pimento or red pepper, sliced cucumber, tomato, hard boiled egg or olives, finely chopped celery leaves or shredded lettuce.

Dishes *must* be served really well chilled. If the weather is warm take the trouble to refrigerate the serving plates for about 30 minutes before putting them on the table. A good martini, after all, should be served in an iced glass, so why shouldn't the same rule apply to cold food?

Do not overdo the gelatine when making cold jellied dishes. A mere 14 g ($\frac{1}{2}$ oz) of powdered gelatine should be enough to set about 570 ml (1 pint) of ingredients unless the weather is very hot indeed.

Turn out fish moulds and mousses by dipping the mould into very hot water, inverting it on to a plate and then tapping the bottom sharply. Return the dish to the refrigerator until ready to serve.

Fish fondues

You probably know all about cheese *fondue*, and the *fondues* you can make where slivers of fillet or rump steak are cooked by your guests at the table over a small burner. But in Japan and other parts of the Far East this same principle is applied to a dish of fish, and sometimes of fish and vegetables, cooked in stock instead of hot oil. A fish *fondue* can make a great talking point for a party. It gets people going, and cooking your own food at a party is always fun.

On one occasion, having what I knew to be a collection of slightly ill-assorted guests coming I decided to have a *fondue* and, since I had plenty of fish but no meat in the refrigerator I settled for a straight fish *fondue*. I cut pieces of filleted mackerel, bass, John Dory and dabs into thin slices and combined them on a plate with some fresh queens. I flavoured the fish with a little lemon juice, salt and white pepper and then left them to marinate for about half an hour. Then I heated the oil on my small table burner until a haze was just rising from it.

There was, as I had expected, a slight constraint among my guests as we sat down to dinner. It was soon forgotten once they began spearing and cooking the pieces of fish they fancied, and the evening quickly turned into one of the most relaxed I ever remember having at Maidenwell.

The fish was almost sea fresh, and I served it with crisp French bread, a large salad and a wide variety of different sauces. As one of the guests said, 'No other way of cooking could have ensured such a swift transition from the raw ingredient to the serving plate.'

If you are feeling rich it would be nice to include some Mediterranean prawns or Dublin Bay prawns in the selection of fish for the *fondue*. But almost as important as the selection of fish is to have a number of colourful, well-flavoured sauces in which to dip the fish. Suitable ones include mustard, chilli, tomato or sweet and sour sauce; and mustard or horseradish mayonnaise. As this fish *fondue* has strong overtones of Japanese and Chinese cooking I always include some plain soy sauce and also some freshly ground ginger and horseradish paste (anything more than the tiniest taste lifts the top of your head off, but the merest pinch does titillate the taste buds).

NOTES ON SERVING A FISH FONDUE

The cooking dish should be large enough for all the guests to use at once. The flame underneath must be adjustable so that you can raise or lower the heat at will. Each guest should be equipped with a suitable implement (it must have a wooden, bone or plastic handle) and you should warn them not to overcook the fish – it will cook in a matter of seconds, not minutes.

In a perfect world each guest has a number of small saucers (the miniature saucers the Chinese use for soy sauce are ideal) to hold the sauces in which the cooked fish is dipped before being eaten. If you don't run to this, divide the sauces into two so that each end of the table has easy access.

Any reasonably good-quality fish is good for this type of dish and the larger the choice the more attractive your *fondue* will be.

Fish soups

These died out almost entirely in this country during the last century, although they still exist around the coasts, mainly among the fishermen's wives who know only too well the economies and nourishment that can be derived from them. But they are now beginning to make a well-merited comeback further inland.

A well-made, aromatic and flavoursome fish soup makes a delicious start to a meal or, if the soup is a hearty one, such as the fish chowders of Newfoundland and New England, it can make an excellent main course in its own right. There is nothing wrong with a main course that one eats with a spoon, unconventional as it may seem. Some of my best *al fresco* parties in Cornwall have been those that started with a mixture of cold meats, crisp raw vegetables and garlic mayonnaise, followed by a rich fish soup served with plenty of crisp French bread and finished by a simple fruit salad.

Determine the character you want a soup to have before you start to cook it. Are you, for instance, going to produce a delicate, ladylike soup, infinitely subtle and elegantly light; or something robust, colourful and hearty? Having taken this decision work around your soup to produce the flavour and strength you are after. A delicate soup should echo the flavour of the fish itself; while with its robust counterpart you can concentrate on an exciting and rich flavouring and leave the fish to provide the texture.

If the soups are to be puréed they must be smooth, and care should be taken to ensure that the finished result has the consistency of liquid velvet or satin. Chunks or flakes of fish should never be overcooked and mushy, and timing in these soups is of paramount importance.

When in doubt undercook rather than overcook the fish so that it has to be removed from the bones by those eating it rather than falling off by itself. Garnish both puréed and whole fish soups with finely chopped parsley, chervil, chives or celery leaves.

Never forget that hot soup must be very hot indeed, and cold soup really well chilled. Nothing is nastier than a tepid 'hot' soup or a slightly warm soup that is meant to be cold.

Foundations and garnishes

Court Bouillon using fish trimmings

Makes about 1.1 litre (2 pints)

White fish trimmings (about 225 g (8 oz))
1 carrot

1 stick celery
2 onions
2 sprigs parsley
1 bay leaf
1 teaspoon salt
½ teaspoon freshly ground black pepper
142 ml (¼ pint) dry white wine

Break up the fish bones and put them in a large saucepan. Clean and chop the carrot. Chop the celery, including the leaves. Peel off the dirty outer skin of the onions but leave the inner skins to add flavour. Combine all the ingredients in the saucepan and cover with cold water. Bring to the boil, cover tightly and simmer for about 1 hour to develop all the flavours. Strain the stock through a sieve lined with two thicknesses of muslin and use as required.

To reduce the stock for making sauces
Turn the strained stock into a clean saucepan, bring to the boil and boil hard until reduced by about one third.

Note: It is very difficult to remember what the volume of stock was when you put it into the saucepan, so I make a small mark with a Chinagraph freezer pencil so I can see how much it has reduced.

Strong fish stock

Made with dry wine or dry cider and fish trimmings, this stock is invaluable for adding flavour to cold dishes like the Fish Mousse on page 181 and also as a basis for certain sauces. You do need a full pint of wine or cider, rather than a mixture with water, in order to give it that extra luxurious flavour.

If a recipe calls for poached fish it should be poached in the stock, which is then strained and used as directed.

It is useful to remember that left-over wines from a

dinner party can be frozen in ice-cube trays and stored in your freezer for later use – it keeps better this way than leaving it for some time in a bottle where it is inclined to go bitter. The fish stock can also be frozen.

Makes 285–570 ml ($\frac{1}{2}$–1 pint)
1 carrot
1 onion
Trimmings from 1.4 kg (3 lb) fish (head, skin, bones, etc.)
4 sprigs parsley
2 bay leaves
Small sprig thyme
Pinch saffron
1 small dried red chilli
Salt and freshly ground black pepper
570 ml (1 pint) dry white wine

Peel and thinly slice the carrot; peel and slice the onion. Place with the fish trimmings, herbs and chilli in a saucepan. Season with a little salt and pepper and pour over the wine. Bring to the boil and simmer very slowly for 30 minutes. Strain the fish stock through muslin or a fine sieve and if necessary return it to the pan and boil hard to reduce to the quantity given in the recipe.

Batters for frying fish

(1) This is an extremely light crisp batter based on the Japanese 'Tempura'. Care should be taken not to overmix the batter which should be lightly beaten with a fork rather than a whisk and this batter should be used fresh, as soon as it has been made, rather than being left to stand. Fish should be cut into thin strips or slices and well dried before being lightly coated with the batter and quickly fried in hot, deep, oil.

90 g (3 oz) plain flour
14 g ($\frac{1}{2}$ oz) cornflour
1 egg
285 ml ($\frac{1}{2}$ pint) water

Combine ingredients, mix lightly with a fork and do not mix again before using. Small lumps will be eradicated during the cooking time. Drain battered fish on kitchen paper as soon as it has been fried.

(2) The classic batter for frying fish used in Italy is one of the best batters I know. It is light and crisp and seems to hold its crispness for longer than most conventional batters. For the best results use the batter as soon as it has been made.

100 g (4 oz) plain flour
3 tablespoons olive oil
Pinch salt
142 ml ($\frac{1}{4}$ pint) water at blood temperature
1 egg white

Combine the flour, oil, salt and water and whisk until smooth. Beat the egg white until stiff and fold it into the batter just before using.

GARNISHES

Being mainly white, most fish benefits from a garnish of some kind; but this should always complement the flavour of the fish, and not be a meaningless frill. Lemon slices and wedges are classic, of course, adding a pleasantly sharp tang; almost any finely chopped fresh herbs will add both flavour and colour. Watercress is particularly good with cold fish. Anchovy fillets, used with caution as they are very strong-flavoured, look very decorative split and arranged in a criss-cross pattern.

But to my mind the most exciting garnish of all is deep-fried parsley. Take quite large sprigs, well dried if they have had to be washed, plunge into hot oil and cook for only about a minute, by which time they will have crisped up and be cooked through. Use to garnish any fried fish dish.

Fish soups fresh from the sea

*Rich aromatic brews which can make a meal in their own right;
light, delicate and subtle soups with a sophistication that
enables them to grace any meal; and straightforward coast-
fresh concoctions to please everyone in the family.*

Scandinavian Fish Chowder

As a child, one summer I was taken on a camping holiday to
Finland. The midnight sun shone and although the food
was relatively simple we lived like kings. Fish was plentiful
and usually flavoured with dill; even now whenever I pick
the dill in my garden I am transported back to that en-
chanted summer.

Serves 6

1 large onion
340 g (12 oz) potatoes
285 g (10 oz) firm-fleshed fish (such as coley, or better
   still huss or monk fish)
57 g (2 oz) butter
1.4 litres (2½ pints) chicken stock
1 tablespoon finely chopped dill
285 ml (½ pint) sour cream
Salt and white pepper
1 tablespoon finely chopped parsley

Peel and very thinly slice the onion and divide into rings.
Peel and dice the potatoes. Cut the fish into 25-mm (1-in)
pieces. Heat the butter in a large heavy saucepan, add the
onion and potatoes and cook over a low heat until almost all
the butter has been absorbed (stir every now and then). Add
the stock, bring to the boil and simmer for 15 minutes. Add
the fish and dill and cook for a further 10–15 minutes until
the ingredients are all tender. Add the cream, bring to the
boil and season. Pour into serving bowls and sprinkle over
the parsley before serving.

Serve with plenty of hot French bread and butter or with garlic bread.

Simple White Fish Chowder

This is a rich soup stew for the winter; warming, nourishing and full of goodness. Serve with hot salt crackers.

Serves 6

113 g (4 oz) salt pork or very fat bacon
2 onions
675 g (1½ lb) potatoes
900 g (2 lb) coley or other firm white fish fillets
1 stick celery
850 ml (1½ pints) chicken or fish stock or water
Salt and freshly ground black pepper
425 ml (¾ pint) milk
28 g (1 oz) butter

Rinse and dry the pork, remove the rind and cut the meat into small dice. Peel and chop the onions. Peel the potatoes and cut into small dice. Cut the fish into 25-mm (1-in) squares. Chop the celery stalk and finely chop the leaves.

Place the meat in a large heavy pan and cook over a medium heat, stirring to prevent sticking, until the fat has melted. Lower the heat, add the onion and continue to cook until the onion is soft and transparent. Add the potatoes and celery and pour over the boiling water or stock. Cook over a high heat for 10 minutes. Add the fish, season, lower the heat and continue to cook for a further 5–10 minutes or until the ingredients are tender. Mix in the milk and butter, heat through and serve at once.

Cream of Parsnip and Coley Soup

If you like the flavour of parsnips this is definitely a soup for you. The flavour of the parsnips is not too pronounced, while the coley adds a subtle extra taste and gives a marvellous texture.

Serves 4

675 g (1½ lb) parsnips
1 onion
850 ml (1½ pints) water and 1 chicken stock cube
570 ml (1 pint) milk
3 bay leaves
450 g (1 lb) coley
1 carton yoghurt
Salt and pepper
2 tablespoons finely chopped parsley

Peel and roughly chop the parsnips. Peel and chop the onion. Combine the parsnips, onion, stock, milk and bay leaves in a saucepan, bring to the boil and cook until the parsnips are tender. Add the fish and simmer gently until it is cooked through. Remove the bay leaves, skin the fish and remove any bones and purée the soup in a liquidiser, through a food mill or in a food processor.

Return the soup to a clean pan, mix in the yoghurt, season and heat through without boiling. Mix in the finely chopped parsley just before serving.

Mushroom and Cucumber Soup with Fish Balls

You will find some strange and maybe new recipes and ideas in this book. This is just such a recipe. It is a subtle blend of mushrooms, lightly cooked, and cucumber; it makes an excellent summer soup or a light starter to precede a rich main course. The *pièce de résistance* is the fish balls made from pure fish which add both flavour, interest and a delicate texture to the soup. The soup is based on a recipe from the Far East where soups are very 'feminine' and subtle.

Serves 4

340 g (12 oz) fish (white firm fish such as coley, saithe,
    huss, etc.)
Salt and freshly ground black pepper
1 small cucumber
85 g (3 oz) very firm button mushrooms
1.1 litres (2 pints) fish stock (see p. 67), or chicken
    stock
1 tablespoon soy sauce
1 tablespoon finely chopped celery or coriander leaves

Mince the fish twice through the fine blades of a mincing machine or purée in a liquidiser or food processor. Season with salt and pepper and refrigerate until firm. Shape the fish into marble-sized balls with the hands and return them to the refrigerator.

Peel and very, very thinly slice the flesh of the cucumber. Very thinly slice the mushrooms.

Bring the stock to the boil, add the fish balls and simmer for 5 minutes. Add the mushrooms and cucumber and continue to cook for a further 15–20 minutes or until the fish balls are cooked and tender. Add the soy sauce, check seasoning and sprinkle over the celery leaves or coriander before serving.

Fishing Boat Soup

I had this late one night made with red mullet that had just been landed on the Cornish coast. The fish were still glistening from the sea when I cooked them and the soup meal was substantial enough for us to need nothing except fruit and cheese to follow it.

Serves 6

6 small red mullet
2 onions
1.7 litres (3 pints) water

1 bouquet garni
2 bay leaves
Salt and freshly ground black pepper
57 g (2 oz) butter
2 tablespoons flour
2 cloves garlic
2 tablespoons oil
2 tablespoons brandy
142 ml ($\frac{1}{4}$ pint) cream
2 tablespoons finely chopped parsley

Clean the mullet and reserve the livers. Remove the heads and tails and cut the fish into 25-mm (1-in) pieces. Peel the onions.

Combine the fish heads and tails in a saucepan with the water, bouquet garni and bay leaves. Add one of the onions, quartered, and season. Bring to the boil, cover and boil for 30 minutes over a high heat. Strain the stock (there should be about 1.4 litres (2$\frac{1}{2}$ pints) by now). Melt three-quarters of the butter, add the flour and mix well. Gradually add the stock, stirring continually over a medium high heat until the soup is thick and smooth.

Very finely chop the second onion. Peel and crush the garlic. Heat the oil and remaining butter in a large heavy pan. Add the onion and garlic and cook over a low heat, stirring, until the onion and garlic are soft and transparent. Add the fish pieces and the livers, raise the heat and cook quickly for a minute on both sides. Add the brandy, set it alight and shake the pan until the flames die down. Pour over the thickened stock, bring to the boil and simmer for 3 minutes. Add the cream, check seasoning and heat through without boiling. Remove the fish with a slotted spoon, dividing it between six bowls, pour over the soup and sprinkle with parsley before serving.

Note: You can fillet the fish and use the bones for stock. Clean the fish and prepare into fillets reserving the liver. Combine the bones and the heads and tails with the water, etc., and continue as before. The fillets should be cut into 50-mm (2-in) thick strips.

Paprika's Fish Chowder 1

I finished this book in Bermuda where I went for a holiday after a dreary spell in hospital. I tried every major restaurant on the island and some of my happiest memories are of the traditional Bermudan chowder, a rich fish soup very reminiscent of Mediterranean soups, aromatic and savoury.

When I returned to a chilly Cornwall I tried to re-create the flavour of those soups and although mine were not quite the same, these two (the first is almost a meal in itself and the second lighter and rather more subtle) transport me almost immediately to that lovely gay island.

Serves 4–6

450 g (1 lb) coley, pollock or other white fish
10 large mussels, clams, large prawns or other shellfish (you can use tinned mussels or tinned chopped clams)
113 g (4 oz) streaky bacon
1 clove garlic
1 onion
3 potatoes
450 g (1 lb) tomatoes
1 tablespoon oil
3 tablespoons finely chopped parsley
1.1 litres (2 pints) stock (include any liquid from the shellfish)
Salt and freshly ground pepper
A pinch of paprika and a pinch of thyme

Cut the fish into bite-sized pieces. Remove the rinds and chop the bacon rashers. Peel and crush the garlic; peel and finely chop the onion. Peel the potatoes and cut into small dice. Peel the tomatoes, remove core and seeds and dice the flesh.

Heat the oil in a large pan, add the bacon and cook over a low heat until the fat runs. Remove with a slotted spoon, add the fish to the juices in the pan and cook over a high heat for just a few seconds until golden. Remove the fish and keep on one side.

Return the bacon to the pan with the onion and garlic and cook over a low heat, stirring to prevent sticking, until the onion is soft and transparent. Add the potatoes and mix over a low heat until the fat in the pan has nearly all been absorbed. Add the tomatoes and parsley, mix well and pour over the stock. Season and add a pinch of paprika and thyme. Bring to the boil and simmer gently until the vegetables are cooked. Add the fish and shellfish, heat through and serve at once.

Note: If the soup is too thick for your liking or if you want to give it an even richer texture add some milk or single cream when re-heating.

Paprika's Fish Chowder 2

This makes use of that delicious vegetable the Jerusalem artichoke. If they are not in season you can make the soup with a purée of parsnips or of leeks and potatoes.

Serves 4–6

340 g ($\frac{3}{4}$ lb) Jerusalem artichokes
1 onion
2 sticks celery
450 g (1 lb) pollock or other firm-fleshed white fish
14 g ($\frac{1}{2}$ oz) butter
1$\frac{1}{2}$ tablespoons flour
1.1 litres (2 pints) fish or chicken stock
Salt and white pepper
2 tablespoons cream
2 tablespoons sherry or dry Vermouth
Paprika

Peel the artichokes (or you can boil them whole and then rub off the skins when they have cooled a bit). Cover the artichokes, onion and chopped celery with cold water, add a little salt and boil until tender.

Steam the fish until it is tender (see page 60), remove any skin and bones and roughly flake the flesh.

Strain the vegetables and purée them through a fine sieve, a food mill or in a liquidiser or food processor.

Melt the butter, add the flour and mix well. Gradually mix in the stock, stirring continually over a medium high heat until the soup comes to the boil and is thick and smooth. Add the purée and mix until the soup is smooth. Season, add the cream and sherry and mix in the flaked fish. Heat through without boiling and sprinkle each serving with a tiny dusting of paprika.

Cream Soup Melissader

I have a writer friend who is genuinely impoverished. Daily she walks on a knife edge between making ends meet and bankruptcy, and yet she produces food on a ridiculously small budget that would please the gods. This soup is one of hers. It was rich, velvety and enormously comforting on a cold winter's evening, and I was quite unable to guess that it is based on coley and root vegetables.

Serves 6

450 g (1 lb) potatoes
225 g ($\frac{1}{2}$ lb) swede
1 onion
43 g ($1\frac{1}{2}$ oz) butter
1.1 litres (2 pints) milk
1 chicken stock cube
3 bay leaves
450 g (1 lb) coley (skinned)
142 ml ($\frac{1}{4}$ pint) single cream
Salt and white pepper
Finely chopped parsley

Peel and roughly chop the potatoes and swede. Peel and chop the onion. Melt the butter, add the vegetables and cook over a very low heat, stirring to prevent sticking, until the butter has been absorbed. Add the milk, crumbled stock cube and bay leaves, bring to the boil, add the coley cut into pieces and simmer for about 15 minutes or until the vegetables are tender. Puréc and return to a clean pan.

Add the cream, season with salt and pepper and, if necessary, a little chicken stock (the soup should be the consistency of velvety cream). Heat through without boiling, pour into serving dishes and sprinkle with finely chopped parsley.

Mullet and Red Fish Soup

The red fish provides the body for this soup while the mullet gives flavour. As after most of these more robust soups the following course should be a light one.

Serves 6

680–900 g ($1\frac{1}{2}$–2 lb) red fish
2 small red mullet
6 tablespoons olive or sunflower oil
142 ml ($\frac{1}{4}$ pint) dry white wine
850 ml ($1\frac{1}{2}$ pints) fish stock (see page 67)
1 onion
2 cloves garlic
2 tablespoons finely chopped parsley
3 tablespoons tomato purée
$2\frac{1}{2}$ tablespoons white wine vinegar
Salt and freshly ground black pepper

Clean the fish (reserve the mullet livers) and remove the heads and tails to make a stock (see page 67). Cut the fish into 50-mm (2-in) pieces.

Heat the oil in a heavy saucepan, add the fish, pour over the wine and add 285 ml ($\frac{1}{2}$ pint) stock. Bring slowly to the boil and simmer for about 5 minutes over a low heat or until the fish is almost cooked through. Remove the fish with a slotted spoon.

Peel and finely chop the onion. Peel and crush the garlic. Add the onion, garlic and parsley to the liquid in the pan with the remaining stock. Bring to the boil, stir in the tomato purée, cover and simmer for 30 minutes, stirring every now and then.

Remove the lid and boil fiercely for about 5 minutes to reduce the liquid slightly. Add the fish and vinegar, check the seasoning and simmer for a further 5 minutes to finish cooking the fish. Put the fish on to four serving dishes, pour over the soup and serve at once.

Leek, Potato and Crab Soup

Serves 4

340 g (12 oz) potatoes, peeled
3 leeks
43 g (1½ oz) butter
570 ml (1 pint) chicken stock
57 g (2 oz) brown crab meat and 57 g (2 oz) white crab meat
285 ml (½ pint) milk
Salt and freshly ground black pepper
Pinch of cayenne
142 ml (¼ pint) single cream
1 tablespoon finely chopped parsley or chives

Dice the potatoes. Clean and thinly slice the leeks. Melt the butter, add the leeks and potatoes and cook over a low heat until the leeks are transparent and the butter has been absorbed. Add the stock, bring to the boil and simmer until the potatoes are soft. Purée the soup through a sieve, a fine food mill, in a liquidiser or a food processor.

Add a little of the soup to the brown crab meat and beat

until smooth. Combine the crab and the purée in a clean pan and mix in the milk. Bring to the boil and season with salt, pepper and a little cayenne. Add the white crab meat and cream and sprinkle the soup with finely chopped parsley or chives before serving.

Note: For a richer soup add a little double cream and a little sherry to the finished soup.

Greek Soup

It is a long time since I was in Greece but I still remember with the utmost clarity sitting in a harbour restaurant just outside Athens and eating a delicious soup that tasted something like this.

Serves 6

900 g (2 lb) firm white fish (coley, bass, bream, brill, etc.)
1.4 litres (2½ pints) *court bouillon* (see page 66) made from the trimmings of the fish with a clove of garlic and 2 chopped leeks
57 g (2 oz) flour
285 ml (½ pint) milk
3 tablespoons tomato purée
1 glass dry white wine
2 tablespoons finely chopped parsley
1 teaspoon finely chopped fresh fennel or dill
1 teaspoon finely grated lemon peel
Salt and freshly ground black pepper

Cut the fish into serving portions. Cover with the cold *court bouillon*, bring slowly to the boil and simmer gently for about 20 minutes or until cooked. Lift the fish out carefully with a slotted spoon.

Mix the flour with the milk to a smooth paste and add with the tomato purée and white wine to the stock in the pan. Bring back to the boil, stirring all the time until the soup is thickened and smooth. Add the herbs and lemon peel, season and return the cooked fish to the soup. Re-heat and serve at once.

Plain and simple or smart and sophisticated, there are fish dishes for every occasion.

Fritto Misto di Mare

Whenever I go to an Italian restaurant I long to eat every-
thing on their astonishingly large menus. In the end I
invariably end up by ordering two of my favourite Italian
foods: mixed seafood salad followed by *fritto misto di mare*.
This is a mixture of fried fish that can have as many as eight
different varieties of fish in it, all crisply fried and very
crunchy. (Deep-fried squid on its own is also delicious.)
The fish must be eaten as soon as possible after they have
been cooked and should be accompanied with quarters of
lemon.

Serves 4

340 g ($\frac{3}{4}$ lb) small squid
225 g ($\frac{1}{2}$ lb) coley or other firm-fleshed white fish
    fillets
2 red mullet
Salt
Flour
Wedges of lemon
Deep oil for frying

Clean the squid (see page 37) and cut the bodies into thin
rings. Cut the coley into thin strips about 13 mm ($\frac{1}{2}$ in)
wide. Clean the mullet (leave in the liver). Remove their
heads and tails and cut each fish into 50-mm (2-in) pieces.

Lightly salt then coat the rings of squid, tentacles, pieces
of coley and red mullet in flour. Heat the oil until a haze rises
from the surface and fry the fish, not too much at a time,
until crisp and golden brown. Drain on kitchen paper and
keep each batch warm until all the fish is cooked.

Pile them on to a white damask napkin and serve at once, garnished with wedges of lemon.

Fried Cutlets of Pollock

Pollock produces marvellous firm-fleshed cutlets and this way of cooking them is unusual and very good indeed. It is rather on the strong and sharp side, and you will find younger children won't like it very much.

Serves 4

4 cutlets of pollock
Salt
4 teaspoons Dijon mustard
Olive or sunflower oil
2 teaspoons lemon juice
1 tablespoon finely chopped capers

Season the cutlets with salt and rub $\frac{1}{2}$ teaspoon of Dijon mustard into each side. Heat some oil in a shallow frying pan, add the cutlets and cook over a moderately high heat until browned on the bottom. Turn them over and fry until brown on the other side. Lower the heat and continue cooking gently until cooked through. Remove on to a serving dish and keep warm. Add the lemon juice and capers, mix well and pour over the fish before serving.

Fried Roach

Roach have to be absolutely fresh; never buy any that have dull and dry skins. If they are really fresh they are delicious cooked in this most simple of all ways.

Serves 4

4 roach
Flour

Salt, pepper and a pinch of cayenne
113 g (4 oz) butter
Lemon wedges

Clean the fish and remove the gills and fins. Season some
flour with salt, pepper and cayenne and coat the fish with
the flour. Clarify the butter (see page 55). Heat the butter
in a large frying pan, add the roach and cook over a medium
heat for about 12 minutes, turning once, until the outside
of the fish is crisp and golden and the inside just cooked
through. Serve with wedges of lemon.

Huss in Curried Cream Sauce

Serves 4

900 g (2 lb) huss
72 g (2½ oz) butter
1 large onion
Flour
Salt and freshly ground black pepper
2 teaspoons curry powder
285 ml (½ pint) single cream

Cut the fish into 50-mm (2-in) pieces. Clarify the butter
(see page 55). Peel and finely chop the onion. Season the
flour with salt and pepper and coat the huss pieces in it.
Heat the butter in a frying pan, add the huss and cook over
a medium heat until golden brown and cooked through.
Remove on to a serving dish and keep warm.

Add the onion to the juices in the pan and cook over a low
heat until the onion is soft, transparent and cooked through.
Add the curry powder and cook for 3 minutes, stirring all
the time. Gradually blend in the cream, stirring over a low
heat until the sauce is hot through – do not allow to boil.
Pour the sauce over the fish and serve with boiled rice and
some poppadums.

Eggs Baked with Fish and Softened Onions

This is based on a Russian dish and it makes a quickly prepared supper. Use any fairly firm-fleshed white fish like pollock, bass or coley. The result is rather like a baked omelette in texture and goes well with a mixed salad and boiled new potatoes.

Serves 4

1 onion
450 g (1 lb) white fish fillets
Seasoned flour
28 g (1 oz) butter
2 tablespoons sunflower oil
4 eggs
Finely chopped parsley or fresh tarragon

Peel and very thinly slice the onion and divide it into rings. Cut the fish fillets (remove the skin if it is tough) into diagonal strips about 13 mm ($\frac{1}{2}$ in) wide. Coat the fish pieces with seasoned flour.

Combine the butter and oil. Add the onion and cook over a low heat until the onion is soft and transparent. Remove the onion, raise the heat and add the fish. Cook until crisp, turning the pieces every now and then. Transfer the fish to a shallow baking dish and smother with the onions.

Beat the eggs lightly, and pour over the onions. Stir lightly with a fork and bake in a fairly hot oven (220 °C (425 °F), Reg. 7) for about 6 minutes or until the eggs are just set. Serve sprinkled with parsley or tarragon.

Strips of Fish in Batter

This is one of my favourite dishes and one I find popular with everyone, especially children. I like to serve it with a rather sharp sauce such as tomato (see page 222) or a highly seasoned tartare sauce or other flavoured mayonnaise (see pages 238–239). It is also surprisingly cheap.

Serves 6

675 g (1½ lb) fish fillets (dabs, whiting, coley, megrim
    sole or any other good white fish)
113 g (4 oz) plain flour
Pinch of salt
1 tablespoon olive or sunflower oil
142 ml (¼ pint) lukewarm pale ale
2 tablespoons lukewarm water
The white of 1 large egg or 2 small ones
Deep oil for frying
Lemon wedges

Remove the skin from the fish and cut the fillets into thin strips about 13 mm (½ in) wide and 50 mm (2 in) long (it is best to cut the fillets diagonally rather than straight across). Dry on kitchen paper.

Whisk the flour and salt to a smooth paste with the oil, beer and water. Leave to stand in a warm place for about 30 minutes, then fold in the stiffly beaten egg whites. Dip the strips of fish into the batter and fry until crisp and golden brown in very hot deep oil. Drain on kitchen paper and keep warm, if necessary, in a moderately hot oven. Serve as soon as possible with wedges of lemon and, if you like, sprigs of crisply fried parsley (see page 69).

Spiced Grey Mullet

Serves 4

4 small or 2 larger grey mullet
2 onions
2 cloves garlic
4 tablespoons vegetable oil
1 tablespoon soy sauce
2 tablespoons water

1 teaspoon soft brown sugar
1 teaspoon lemon juice
Salt, pepper and a pinch of chilli powder

Fillet the fish. Peel and finely chop the onion and garlic. Heat the oil, add the fillets and fry over a very high heat to brown quickly on both sides. Remove the fillets. Add the onions and garlic to the juices in the pan and cook them over a low heat until the onions are soft and transparent. Combine the soy sauce, water, sugar and lemon juice, season with salt and pepper and a pinch of chilli powder and mix well.

Return the fish to the pan with the onions and garlic. Pour over the sauce, bring to the boil and simmer for about 6 minutes or until the fish is just tender. Serve with rice.

Queens Provençal

Serves 4–6

225 g (8 oz) firm button mushrooms
225 g (8 oz) queens
1 small onion
2 cloves garlic
3 tablespoons olive or vegetable oil
1 small tin tomatoes
1 tablespoon tomato purée
Salt and freshly ground black pepper
2 bay leaves
Grated rind and juice of $\frac{1}{2}$ orange
Pinch oregano and thyme
$1\frac{1}{2}$ tablespoons dry Vermouth
57 g (2 oz) butter
85 g (3 oz) fresh white breadcrumbs
2 tablespoons finely chopped parsley

Very thinly slice the mushrooms. Pick over the queens, removing any black veins, and pat dry on kitchen paper. Peel and finely chop the onion. Peel and crush the garlic.

Heat 1 tablespoon of the oil in a small saucepan, add the onion and garlic and cook over a low heat until the onion is soft and transparent. Add the tomatoes and tomato puree, mix well and bring to the boil. Season and add the bay leaves, orange rind and juice, oregano, thyme and Vermouth and simmer for about 30 minutes, removing the lid for the last 10 minutes so that the mixture reduces to a thick rich consistency. Remove the bay leaves.

Melt the butter, add the queens and mushrooms and toss over a high heat for about 3 minutes. Fry the breadcrumbs until crisp in the remaining oil.

Add the queens and mushrooms to the tomato sauce, mix in the parsley and check seasoning. Transfer the mixture to a shallow serving dish or individual ramekins, sprinkle the breadcrumbs over the surface and re-heat, if necessary, for a few minutes in a hot oven.

Crisply Fried River Fish

Some time ago I was doing the cooking for the thirty or so members of my husband's expedition to Borneo. Our diet was rather dreary, consisting mainly of rice or pasta with whatever sauce I could conjure up from the stores. Our highlights were when the locals brought us wild pig, monkey or deer, or when we had fresh fish from the river. These were small and bristling with bones, but delicious cooked like this.

Serves 4

8–12 small river fish such as roach or perch
Flour
Salt and freshly ground black pepper
Deep oil for frying

Scale the fish, remove the heads, tails and fins and cut them, bones and all, into pieces about 50 mm (2 in) wide. Season some flour with salt and pepper, roll the pieces of fish in the seasoned flour and then deep fry them in very hot fat until they are so crisp that the bones have almost been dissolved and the taste is one of delicious crispness rather than actual fish. Drain and serve as quickly as possible with any sauce suitable for fried fish.

Fish Fried in Batter

One thinks at once of fish and chips out of a newspaper, eaten walking home from the cinema and giving off an aroma that takes one back to childhood. Recapturing that obvious taste is largely a matter of getting the batter right, and cooking the fish as quickly as possible. The fat or oil you use must be free from the taste of other foods and at smoking point when you add the battered ingredients.

The batter must not be too thick or it will be heavy and cloying and the food must be well drained on kitchen paper and served at once or the batter will be soggy and un-appetising. Egg white added to the batter will give it a lighter texture; so will beer, and if you add a little baking powder you will find that it keeps crisp for a little longer.

Dip the fish into the batter just before you are going to cook it (the batter itself can be prepared in advance), plunge the ingredients into very hot fat or oil, push them below the surface of the fat to ensure that all surfaces brown evenly and remove with a slotted spoon as soon as the batter is crisp and golden brown. Fish to be cooked in this way should not be too thick or the batter will be cooked before the centre is done.

Do not attempt to cook too much food at one go and as soon as the first batch is cooked, put it on to a well-heated serving dish, lined with kitchen paper, and keep warm in a moderate oven while cooking the remainder.

Garnish foods fried in batter with bunches of deep fried parsley (see page 69) and lemon wedges.

Perch Milanese

Serves 4

8 small perch
142 ml ($\frac{1}{4}$ pint) olive oil
Juice of 1 lemon
Salt and freshly ground black pepper
Flour
2 eggs, beaten
Dry breadcrumbs
72 g ($2\frac{1}{2}$ oz) butter

Fillet and skin the fish and place in a shallow dish. Combine the oil and lemon juice and season it with salt and freshly ground black pepper. Pour the marinade over the fillets and leave them for 2 hours, turning every now and then.

Remove the fillets from the marinade and dry on kitchen paper. Coat in flour and then in beaten eggs and breadcrumbs.

Melt 57 g (2 oz) of the butter in a frying pan, add the fish and cook over a gentle heat until golden and cooked through. Remove on to a heated serving dish. Add the remaining butter to the pan juices and stir over a medium heat until it turns golden brown (do not allow it to burn and turn black). Pour over the perch and serve at once with boiled new potatoes and a salad or green vegetables.

Coley Cutlets

Deliciously crisp cutlets which can be made from coley or any other reasonably cheap white fish.

Serves 4

450 g (1 lb) coley or white fish fillets, skin removed
85 g (3 oz) crustless white bread
Milk
14 g ($\frac{1}{2}$ oz) butter

1 tablespoon finely chopped raw onion
2 egg yolks
Salt and freshly ground black pepper
Dried breadcrumbs
Vegetable oil for frying

Mince the fish through the fine blades of a mincing machine, cover the bread with milk, leave to stand for 5 minutes and squeeze out the excess milk. Combine the minced fish and milk and mix well. (Alternatively you can use a liquidiser or food processor.)

Heat the butter in a pan, add the onion and cook over a low heat until the onion is soft and transparent. Beat the egg yolks until smooth. Add the onion and beaten eggs to the fish and bread mixture, season and mix well.

Dip your hands into cold water and shape the fish mixture into eight small cutlets. Refrigerate for an hour to consolidate their shape and then coat them in breadcrumbs. Fry the cutlets in 13 mm ($\frac{1}{2}$ in) of very hot vegetable oil until golden brown on both sides and drain on kitchen paper before serving

Serve the cutlets with chips or mashed potatoes and a caper or Hollandaise sauce.

Spiced Fried Fish

This is a Malaysian way of cooking fish and if you like spicy food you will find it delicious. Serve the fish with boiled rice and, if you like, with a home-made tomato sauce.

Serves 4

2 red chillies
1 teaspoon ground turmeric
1 teaspoon salt
1 teaspoon lemon juice
450 g (1 lb) coley, pollock or other white fish fillets,
    skin removed
Olive or vegetable oil

Remove the seeds of the chillies and finely chop the flesh. Combine the turmeric, chillies, salt and lemon juice in a pestle and mortar, liquidiser or food processor, and grind it to a paste.

Rub the paste into both sides of the fish fillets and leave to stand in a cool place for 30 minutes. Cut the fish into strips about 13 mm ($\frac{1}{2}$ in) wide.

Heat the oil (6 mm ($\frac{1}{4}$ in) deep) in a heavy frying pan. Add the pieces of fish when the oil is very hot and fry on both sides until tender and slightly crisp. Drain on kitchen paper and pile on to a hot serving plate.

Curried Coley

Other white fish can be used equally well for this dish; look in your fishmonger's and choose the white fish that is the least expensive. Serve with rice and, if you like, a mild curry vegetable dish. The curry ingredients can be bought from good delicatessen shops or shops which specialise in Indian and Oriental ingredients, and coriander can easily be grown in a herb garden.

Serves 4

450 g (1 lb) white fish fillets, skins removed
3 red peppers
1 clove garlic
25 mm (1 in) fresh ginger root
1 teaspoon ground turmeric
3 green chillies (or use dried red chillies)
1 carton yoghurt
1$\frac{1}{2}$ teaspoons salt
1 large onion
4 tablespoons vegetable oil
$\frac{1}{2}$ teaspoon garam masala
2 bay leaves
1 teaspoon dry English mustard

> 1 tablespoon finely chopped fresh coriander or celery
>   leaves
> Lemon wedges

Cut the fish into strips about 13 mm ($\frac{1}{2}$ in) wide. Remove the seeds from the red peppers and chop the flesh. Peel and finely chop the garlic clove and ginger root. Combine the red peppers, garlic, ginger and turmeric and grind to a paste in a pestle and mortar, liquidiser or food processor. Rub the mixture into the fish strips.

Remove the seeds from the green chillies and cut the flesh into very thin strips. Combine them with the yoghurt and mix well, season with salt and mix in the fish strips. Leave to stand for 30 minutes in a cool place.

Peel and very thinly slice the onion and divide into rings. Heat the oil in a heavy frying pan. Add the onion and cook over a low heat until soft and transparent. Add the garam masala, bay leaves and mustard and mix well. Cook for 2 minutes and add the pieces of fish and the liquid they have been marinated in. Cover and cook over a *very* low heat for 10–15 minutes until the fish is just tender (shake the pan every now and then to prevent it sticking to the bottom).

Serve the fish in a circle of boiled rice and garnish with chopped coriander or celery leaves. Accompany it with quarters of lemon or lime.

Fried Fish with Potato Salad

Use any firm-fleshed fish that happens to be inexpensive at the time for this Russian dish. I would suggest coley, huss, pollock, bass, grey mullet or mackerel, and you can also use whitebait or sprats.

> *Serves 5–6*
>
> 675 g (1$\frac{1}{2}$ lb) firm-fleshed white fish or mackerel
>   fillets; or 450 g (1 lb) sprats or whitebait
> 2 eggs, beaten
> Flour

Salt and pepper
450 g (1 lb) potatoes
2 dill pickled cucumbers
2 tablespoons sunflower oil
½ teaspoon mustard
57 g (2 oz) butter
2 tablespoons oil
Lemon wedges

Cut the fish fillets into thick slices. Dip into beaten egg and then into seasoned flour until all sides are well coated.

Cook the potatoes in their skins until tender, drain, cool and skin. Cut both the potatoes and dill pickled cucumber into small dice. Combine the sunflower oil with the mustard and 2 teaspoons of the cucumber liquid and season with salt and pepper. Add the dressing to the potatoes and cucumber and mix lightly.

Melt the butter with 2 tablespoons oil. Add the fish, a few pieces at a time, and cook over a high heat until crisp and golden brown. Drain on kitchen paper and keep warm while frying the rest. Transfer to a heated serving dish, garnish with the potato salad and some lemon wedges and serve at once.

Marinaded and Fried Fillets of Mackerel en Goujon

At certain times of the year in coastal areas mackerel become so plentiful one can tire of the conventional ways of cooking them. Here is something a little different.

Serves 6

8 small fillets mackerel
2 eggs
1 tablespoon oil
Salt and freshly ground black pepper
Flour

113 g (4 oz) fresh white breadcrumbs
Oil for deep frying
Lemon wedges

Marinade
2 carrots
1 onion
425 ml ($\frac{3}{4}$ pint) dry white wine
Juice of 1 lemon
Pinch sage and thyme
1 bay leaf
8 black peppercorns
Pinch salt

Peel and slice the carrots. Peel and slice the onion. Combine the wine, carrots and onion, lemon juice, herbs, peppercorns and salt in a saucepan, bring to the boil and simmer very gently for 15 minutes. Leave to cool.

Cut the fillets into 50–mm (2–in) wide diagonal slices. Pour over the marinade and leave to stand in a cold place for 4 hours.

Drain off the marinade and pat the fish dry on kitchen paper. Beat the eggs until smooth, add the oil, mix well and season. Coat the mackerel slices in flour, dip into beaten egg and then coat them with the breadcrumbs.

Heat the oil until a haze rises and cook the slices of mackerel until crisp and golden brown. Drain on kitchen paper, pile on a napkin and garnish with lemon wedges.

Serve with crisply fried parsley sprigs (see page 69) and Orange, Dubonnet and Horseradish sauce (see page 241).

Huss, Scampi Style

Huss, easy to obtain and not expensive, has a texture remarkably like that of a shellfish. Often it is used (without the eater's knowledge) in place of scampi; but since huss is thoroughly delicious why not serve it *honestly* in many of the ways that scampi are cooked. Suitable accompaniments are chips and salad, rice and tomato sauce, or mashed potatoes and a green vegetable.

Serves 4–5

675 g (1½ lb) huss, skinned and off the bone
2 eggs
Salt
85 g (3 oz) fine brown breadcrumbs
Deep fat for frying
To serve: Quarters of lemon; sauce tartare
Optional garnishing: Fried parsley

Cut the huss into thin strips that resemble a scampi shape 38–50 mm (1½–2 in) long and about 13 mm (½ in) wide and dry on kitchen paper. Beat the eggs with a little salt. Dip the huss pieces in the beaten egg and then roll them in the breadcrumbs until well coated.

Heat the deep fat or oil until smoking and drop in the huss pieces a few at a time. Cook until *just* golden brown (over-cooking ruins the texture). Remove from the oil and drain on kitchen paper. Keep warm while frying the rest of the fish.

Serve as soon as possible with lemon wedges and sauce tartare (see page 239).

Bream in Egg Sauce

Serves 4

900 g (2 lb) bream fillets, skinned
85 g (3 oz) flour
Salt and freshly ground black pepper
57 g (2 oz) butter
2 tablespoons olive or vegetable oil
2 hard-boiled eggs
85 g (3 oz) butter
2 teaspoons lemon juice
1 tablespoon finely chopped parsley
Pinch cayenne pepper

Cut the fish fillets into strips about 50 mm (2 in) wide and coat them in seasoned flour.

Melt the first amount of butter with the oil in a frying pan. Add the fish and cook over a high heat, turning the pieces every now and then, until they are golden brown and the flesh flakes fairly easily. Pile on to a heated serving plate and keep warm while making the sauce.

Chop the hard-boiled eggs. Melt the butter in a small saucepan. Add the lemon juice and parsley, season with salt, pepper and a pinch of cayenne and lightly mix in the hard-boiled eggs. Pour the sauce over the fish and serve at once.

Fillets of John Dory, Megrim Sole or Dabs with Sage

This is an adaptation of an Italian dish made with small sole. I am not saying that the substitutes (except John Dory which is not always easy to get and can be as expensive as sole) are as good as the real thing, but they come a very close second and the strong taste of sage is very attractive on a hot summer evening.

Serves 4

2 eggs
Salt and freshly ground black pepper
8 fillets of John Dory, megrim sole or large dabs
Flour
Dry breadcrumbs
8 fresh sage leaves
Olive or sunflower oil

Beat the eggs until smooth and season them. Dip the fillets in flour, then coat them in beaten egg and finally in dry breadcrumbs. Very finely chop the sage leaves.

Heat about 6 mm ($\frac{1}{4}$ in) oil in a shallow frying pan. Add the fish fillets and the sage and cook until the fillets are golden brown on both sides. Drain on kitchen paper and sprinkle with a little salt. Arrange with the sage on a hot serving dish and serve at once.

Alternative Fish à l'Américaine

Now that lobster has become so outrageously expensive (if ever you can afford one these days you certainly don't mask its flavour in any way) cooking à l'Américaine comes into its own as the perfect foil for good-textured fish of all kinds. Monk fish are perhaps the best of all, since their flesh is already considerably like that of lobster, firm, slightly 'springy' and very succulent. You can also use other firm-fleshed fish: sea bass or skate, taken off the bone and cut into strips. This is an extravagant dish, but you can always console yourself with the fact that you are not using lobster as a base.

Serves 6

1.4 kg (3 lb) white fish off the bone
Flour
Salt and freshly ground black pepper
Pinch cayenne
3 onions
2 cloves garlic
1 396-g (14-oz) tin tomatoes
4 tablespoons olive or sunflower oil
3 tablespoons brandy
425 ml ($\frac{3}{4}$ pint) dry white wine
Pinch thyme and marjoram
2 bay leaves
1 tablespoon tomato purée
Tabasco sauce
3 tablespoons double cream

Cut the fish into slices about 6 mm ($\frac{1}{4}$ in) thick (with a really firm fish I cut the slices to resemble the medallions cut from the body of a lobster). Season the flour with salt, pepper and cayenne and dust the fish with it. Peel and finely chop the onions, peel and crush the garlic, chop the tomatoes.

Heat the oil in a large, deep frying pan. Add the onions and garlic and cook over a low heat, stirring now and then until the onions become soft and transparent. Remove the onions with a slotted spoon. Raise the heat, add the fish to the juices in the pan and cook over a high heat, turning the slices once gently, until lightly browned on both sides. Add half the brandy, bring it to the boil and set it on fire. Shake the pan until the flames die down and immediately remove the fish.

Return the onions and garlic to the pan and add the wine, tomatoes, herbs, bay leaves, tomato purée and a few drops Tabasco sauce. Bring to the boil, and cook, uncovered, over a fairly high heat for about 30 minutes or until the sauce is thick (it should be the consistency of a thin vegetable purée).

Remove bay leaves, add the fish and remaining brandy to the sauce, check the seasoning and simmer for 5 minutes or until the fish is just cooked. Add the cream and heat through without boiling.

Serve the fish and sauce in the centre of a rice ring and garnish with plenty of finely chopped parsley and, if you want to do the thing in style, crescents of crisply fried bread or puff pastry.

Coley with Almond and Yoghurt Sauce

Fillets of bass would also be good with this unusual sauce. A liquidiser or food processor is needed to make it.

Serves 6

900 g (2 lb) coley or bass fillets
1 teaspoon ground turmeric
Salt and freshly ground black pepper
4 onions
57 g (2 oz) butter
1 stick cinnamon (about 50 mm (2 in) long)

425 ml ($\frac{3}{4}$ pint) milk
225 g (8 oz) ground almonds
285 ml ($\frac{1}{2}$ pint) yoghurt

Remove the skin from the fillets and cut them across into pieces about 50 mm (2 in) wide. Sprinkle with the turmeric and season.

Peel and finely chop the onions. Melt the butter in a frying pan. Add the onions and cinnamon stick and cook over a low heat until the onions are soft and transparent. Add the fish, raise the heat, brown the fish quickly and then pour in the milk. Bring to the boil, lower the heat and simmer gently for about 5 minutes.

Reduce the almonds to a paste in a liquidiser or food processor. Add the yoghurt, a spoonful at a time, to get a creamy paste. Pour the yoghurt mixture over the fish, cover and continue to simmer gently for 10 minutes.

Remove the cinnamon and serve with saffron-flavoured rice.

Turkish Spiced Fish

In Turkey this is made with swordfish, but any reasonably firm-fleshed fish will do.

Serves 6

900 g (2 lb) firm-fleshed white fish fillets
850 ml ($1\frac{1}{2}$ pints) water
1 tablespoon white wine vinegar
2 cloves garlic
1 small piece ginger root, sliced
Pinch ground saffron
1 teaspoon dry English mustard
2 teaspoons curry powder
2 onions
2 green chillies
2 tablespoons olive oil
1 tablespoon soft brown sugar
2 spring onions

Remove the skin and cut the fish into serving-sized portions. Place the fish in a shallow pan, cover with the cold water and vinegar, season and bring slowly to the boil. Simmer gently for about 10 minutes or until the fish is just tender. Drain, reserving the liquid.

Pound the garlic, sliced ginger, saffron and mustard to a smooth paste in a pestle and mortar. Blend in the curry powder and add 4 tablespoons of the liquid in which the fish was cooked.

Place the cooked fish in a dish, spread over the spiced mixture and leave to stand in a cool place for 15 minutes.

Peel and thinly slice the onions and divide into rings. Halve the chillies, remove the seeds and stalk and cut the flesh into very thin strips. Heat the oil in a frying pan, add the onions and chilli and cook over a low heat for 5 minutes, stirring every now and then. Add the fish and continue to cook over a low heat for a further 10 minutes, turning once during the cooking time. Sprinkle with sugar and chopped spring onions and serve with rice and a salad.

Fish Balls with a Curry Flavour

These curried fish balls make excellent 'nibbles' to go with drinks when you really want to put yourself out to entertain people.

> 1 small onion
> 450 g (1 lb) firm-fleshed white fish like coley fillets
> 2 tablespoons finely chopped parsley
> Salt and freshly ground black pepper
> 1 teaspoon garam masala
> 1 tablespoon lemon juice
> 2 eggs, beaten
> Dried breadcrumbs
> Deep oil for frying

Peel and mince the onion. Steam the fish until tender. Discard the skin and any bones and pound the fish with the onion (or pass both through the fine blades of a mincing machine). Add the parsley, season and mix in the garam masala and lemon juice. Chill the mixture and shape it into neat walnut-sized balls with your hands. Dip in beaten egg, roll in dried breadcrumbs and then fry for a few minutes in very hot oil until golden brown. Drain on kitchen paper.

Serve the fish balls on cocktail sticks with a sharp sauce such as tomato, prawn or tartare.

Skate in Black Butter

This is perhaps the most classic of all ways to cook skate wings. It is good but it has to be made with very fresh fish and should only be made from the centre cut from the larger skate wings.

Serves 4

4 pieces of skate wings
Court bouillon (see page 66)
72 g ($2\frac{1}{2}$ oz) butter
$1\frac{1}{2}$ tablespoons white wine vinegar
1 tablespoon capers, finely chopped
2 tablespoons finely chopped parsley

Place the skate wings in a shallow pan, cover with *court bouillon* and bring gently to the boil, turning down the heat immediately any bubbles appear on the surface. Simmer very gently for about 10–15 minutes until the flesh of the wings is opaque and will just flake from the bones. Transfer to a serving dish. Melt the butter in a frying pan and cook over a medium heat until golden (do not allow it to blacken). Pour the butter over the fish. Pour the vinegar into the pan and stir until it boils, then pour over the fish. Sprinkle with the chopped capers and parsley and serve at once.

Fried Skate Espagnole

Serves 4

Espagnole sauce (see page 224)
Flour
Salt and freshly ground black pepper
4 skate wings, about 225 g (8 oz) each
57 g (2 oz) butter
2 tablespoons oil

Make the Espagnole sauce. Season some flour and coat the skate wings in it. Heat the butter with the oil in a large frying pan. Add the skate wings and cook over a medium high heat for about 4 minutes on each side until the flesh of the wings becomes opaque and just flakes from the bones.

Arrange on a serving dish and keep warm. Add the Espagnole sauce to the juices in the pan, mix well and bring to the boil. Pour over the fish and serve at once.

Huss with Green Pepper and Lettuce

At certain times of the year, however carefully we plan our garden, there are far more lettuces than any normal family can cope with. As a result I try out a great number of recipes geared to making good use of them. This is one of the breakthroughs; it really works and is well worth making even if you don't happen to have lettuces going begging.

Serves 4

675 g ($1\frac{1}{2}$ lb) huss or any other firm-fleshed white fish
1 lettuce
1 green pepper
42 g ($1\frac{1}{2}$ oz) butter
$\frac{1}{2}$ teaspoon mustard
Pinch turmeric
142 ml ($\frac{1}{4}$ pint) double cream.

Cut the fish into thin strips about 13 mm ($\frac{1}{2}$ in) wide and 50 mm (2 in) long. Clean and shred the lettuce. Remove the core and seeds of the pepper and thinly slice the flesh.

Blanch the pepper strips in boiling salted water for 5 minutes and drain well.

Melt the butter, add the lettuce and pepper strips and cook over a low heat, stirring to prevent browning, for 5 minutes. Add the fish and continue cooking, stirring every now and then, for about 6 minutes or until the fish is just cooked through. Add the mustard, turmeric and cream and mix well. Simmer over a low heat without boiling for 5 minutes and serve with rice and a green salad.

Conger Eel Steaks

Conger eel steaks are not quite tender enough to grill but they can be fried and make a quick and very acceptable meal.

Serves 4

675 g ($1\frac{1}{2}$ lb) potatoes
Knob of butter
2 tablespoons double cream
Salt and freshly ground black pepper
4 conger eel steaks cut from the head end of the eel, about 38 mm ($1\frac{1}{2}$ in) thick
28 g (1 oz) butter
2 tablespoons oil
2 teaspoons flour
1 tablespoon capers
142 ml ($\frac{1}{4}$ pint) dry cider
Sprigs of parsley

Boil the potatoes and mash until smooth, beating in the butter and the cream. Season and spread out on a shallow serving dish. Keep warm while cooking the fish. Remove any fins from the eel. Heat the butter and oil, add the steaks and cook gently for about 10 minutes a side until the fish is beginning to flake from the bone. Arrange on the potatoes and keep warm.

Add the flour, capers and cider to the juices in the pan, season, bring to the boil and cook over a high heat, stirring, until the sauce is reduced by about half. Pour over the eel, garnish with sprigs of parsley and serve with a vegetable such as carrots Vichy or slices of beetroot cooked in a cheese sauce.

Smoked Mackerel Kedgeree

This is so rich and flavoursome that I serve it as a supper or luncheon dish rather than for breakfast, with a green salad and French bread.

Serves 4

2 smoked mackerel
1 small onion
57 g (2 oz) butter
1 tablespoon olive oil
170 g (6 oz) long-grain rice
2 hard-boiled eggs
4 tablespoons cream
1 egg
Salt and white pepper
Finely chopped parsley
Cayenne pepper (optional)

Remove the skin and bones from the mackerel and flake the fish. Peel and chop the onion. Heat 28 g (1 oz) of the butter and the oil in a heavy pan, add the onion and cook over a low heat until soft and transparent. Add the rice and stir until the rice is transparent. Add enough cold water to come about 19 mm ($\frac{3}{4}$ in) above the level of the rice. Bring to the boil, stir once, cover tightly and cook over a low heat, without stirring, for about 20 minutes or until the water has been absorbed and the rice grains are just tender. Stir with a fork to separate the rice.

Add the flaked fish and the hard-boiled eggs, cut into quarters, to the rice and dot with the remaining butter.

Beat the cream with the egg until smooth. Pour this mixture over the rice, season and lightly mix in. Cook over a low heat, stirring very gently, until the rice is coated with the creamy sauce. Serve at once with a sprinkling of finely chopped parsley and, if you like, a little dusting of cayenne over the surface.

Fishcakes

I have made good fishcakes from all kinds of fish; leftover cooked fish, the most expensive and the cheapest. Salmon fishcakes, served with Hollandaise sauce, are so good they are worthy of a dinner party; fishcakes made from conger eel are delicious in their own right and make a good supper dish. I like to serve the more common or garden fishcakes with a home-made tomato sauce or some other well-flavoured sauce.

Serves 4

225 g (8 oz) cooked and flaked fish
450 g (1 lb) cooked and mashed potato
14 g ($\frac{1}{2}$ oz) melted butter
Salt and freshly ground black pepper
2 eggs, beaten
Dry white breadcrumbs
Oil and butter to fry

Pound or mince the fish until fairly smooth. Add the mashed potato and melted butter, season and work until the mixture is firm. Shape into cakes about 19 mm ($\frac{3}{4}$ in) thick and about 75 mm (3 in) across, dip into beaten egg and then into breadcrumbs and chill for 30 minutes. Give the cakes a second coating of egg and breadcrumbs and fry in a mixture of oil and butter until golden brown and crisp on both sides.

Variations

Give your fishcakes extra flavour by adding any of the following ingredients, or a mixture of two or more.

Pinch dried herbs; 1 tablespoon finely chopped parsley, chives or chervil; some finely chopped anchovy fillets; anchovy essence, Worcestershire sauce or Tabasco sauce; freshly grated horseradish or mustard powder; finely chopped sautéed onion; a little crisply-fried crumbled bacon.

Poached fish

This is the delicate way of cooking fish, to a point of the most perfect tenderness. Poached fish presents itself as an ideal foil for the most exciting of sauces.

Fish in Paprika and Sour Cream

Serves 6

900 g (2 lb) mackerel, coley or whiting fillets
Salt
2 large onions
85 g (3 oz) lard
1 tablespoon paprika
1 teaspoon flour
142 ml ($\frac{1}{4}$ pint) water
285 ml ($\frac{1}{2}$ pint) sour cream
1 tablespoon finely chopped parsley

Cut the fish into 25-mm (1-in) wide slices and season with salt. Put on one side while preparing the other ingredients.

Peel and thinly slice the onions and divide into rings. Melt the lard in a shallow frying pan. Add the onions and cook over a low heat, stirring every now and then, for about 5 minutes until golden and transparent. Sprinkle over the paprika and flour and mix well. Gradually mix in 142 ml ($\frac{1}{4}$ pint) water and cook, covered, for 15 minutes. Place the fish slices on top, cover and continue to cook over a low heat for 15 minutes. Mix in the sour cream, stir gently without breaking up the fish and cook for a further 5 minutes or until the fish is cooked. Transfer the fish and onions to a serving plate; stir the juices in the pan and pour them over.

Garnish with finely chopped parsley and serve with boiled potatoes. If red peppers are in season the dish can be garnished with thinly cut rings of pepper, seeds removed.

Marietta's Coley Stew

A delicious concoction, this falls between two stools, too
thick to be called a soup and really a little too liquid to be
called a stew. It is rich and aromatic and makes a filling
main course.

Serves 4

900 g (2 lb) coley fillet
570 ml (1 pint) *court bouillon* (see page 66)
1 onion
1 clove garlic
2 sticks celery
2 tablespoons olive or sunflower oil
Pinch saffron
1 792-g (28-oz) tin tomatoes
Salt and freshly ground black pepper
Bouquet garni
1 small loaf French bread
Oil for frying
2 tablespoons finely chopped parsley

Remove the skin from the coley and cut the fish into
50-mm (2-in) squares. Put the fish into a heavy pan, add the
court bouillon, bring gently to the boil and simmer for
about 10 minutes until just cooked. Strain the liquid in the
pan and reserve it. Put the fish to one side.

Peel and finely chop the onion. Peel and crush the garlic.
Remove the leaves from the celery and thinly slice the
stalks. Heat the olive or sunflower oil, add the onion, garlic
and celery and cook over a low heat, stirring every now and
then, until the onion is soft and transparent. Infuse the
saffron in 2 tablespoons of warm water. Add the tomatoes
to the pan and mix well to break up. Season, add the bouquet
garni, saffron and reserved liquid, bring to the boil, cover
and simmer for 20 minutes.

Cut the French bread into 13-mm ($\frac{1}{2}$-in) thick slices and fry them in oil until golden brown on both sides; drain off any excess on kitchen paper.

Add the fish to the tomato mixture and heat through. Arrange slices of fried bread in four serving dishes and cover with the fish removed from the liquid with a slotted spoon; pour over the liquid. Sprinkle over the finely chopped parsley and serve at once.

Fish Goulash

This rich robust dish with a delicious flavouring of paprika is, as you can imagine, a Hungarian dish. It should be served with boiled potatoes and a cabbage of some kind.

Serves 4

900 g (2 lb) firm white fillets (the imported carp is good for this, so is coley and huss and I have also made it with conger eel)
Salt
2 onions
42 g ($1\frac{1}{2}$ oz) butter
1 tablespoon paprika
Red wine
3 bay leaves

Cut the fish into pieces about 50 mm (2 in) square. Season with salt. Peel and thinly slice the onions and divide them into rings. Melt the butter, add the onion and cook over a low heat until the onions are golden brown. Add the paprika and mix well. Place the fish on top and add just enough red wine to cover. Top with the bay leaves, bring to the boil, cover and simmer very slowly for about 20 minutes.

Remove the fish to a heated serving dish, cover with the onions and pour over the sauce.

Monk Fish with Wine Sauce

Serves 6

900 g (2 lb) monk fish
2 onions
3 carrots
2 sticks celery
2 cloves garlic
42 g (1½ oz) butter
2 tablespoons vinegar
142 ml (¼ pint) white wine
142 ml (¼ pint) water
570 ml (1 pint) *court bouillon* (see page 66)
2 tablespoons finely chopped parsley
Pinch of thyme
142 ml (¼ pint) double cream
Salt and freshly ground black pepper

Cut the monk fish into scampi-sized pieces (about 13 mm (½ in) thick and 38 mm (1½ in) long. Peel and chop the onions. Peel the carrots and cut into small dice. Very thinly slice the celery. Peel and crush the garlic.

Melt the butter, add the onion, garlic, carrot and celery and cook over a low heat until the onion is soft and transparent. Add the wine, water and *court bouillon* and boil over a high heat until the vegetables are soft. Add the monk fish and simmer gently for 6 minutes or until just tender. Sprinkle in the chopped parsley and thyme, stir in the cream and season. Serve with rice and a salad.

Stewed Perch or Roach with Rich Cream Sauce

You can also make this with fillets of whiting or other fish that are cheap but do not have a very definite flavour of their own; this is provided by the sauce.

Serves 6

900 g (2 lb) perch or roach
1 onion
2 green or red peppers
285 ml ($\frac{1}{2}$ pint) water
285 ml ($\frac{1}{2}$ pint) white wine
Salt and freshly ground black pepper
Bouquet garni
2 bay leaves
28 g (1 oz) cornflour
285 ml ($\frac{1}{2}$ pint) single cream
2 egg yolks
14 g ($\frac{1}{2}$ oz) paprinka

Fillet the fish and remove their skins (unless very small and tender). Cut the fish into diagonal slices about 50 mm (2 in) wide. Peel and thinly slice the onion and divide into rings. Remove the core and seeds of the peppers and cut the flesh into thin strips.

Place the fish in a saucepan with the onion and pepper. Pour over the water and wine, season and add the bouquet garni and bay leaves Bring to the boil, cover tightly and simmer gently for about 20–25 minutes until the vegetables and fish are cooked. Strain off the cooking liquid and remove the bouquet garni and bay leaves. Arrange the fish on a heated serving dish and keep warm.

Transfer the cooking liquid to a saucepan. Bring it to the boil and cook over a high heat until reduced to one third. Mix the cornflour to a paste with the cream and beat in the egg yolks. Add the mixture to the cooking liquid and cook over a moderate heat, stirring all the time, until the sauce is thick and satiny. Season the sauce with salt, pepper and half the paprika. Pour the sauce over the fish and sprinkle over the remaining paprika.

Savoy Queens

This is a delicious little dish flavoured, rather unusually for fish, with a little thyme. If you don't like the idea of thyme with fish, substitute a little tarragon or chervil.

Serves 4

450 g (1 lb) queens
57 g (2 oz) firm button mushrooms
42 g (1½ oz) butter
2 tablespoons flour
285 ml (½ pint) fish stock (see page 67)
142 ml (¼ pint) home-made mayonnaise (see page 237)
½ teaspoon fresh thyme leaves
Salt and freshly ground black pepper

Pick over the queens, removing any black veins. Thinly slice the mushrooms. Melt one-third of the butter in a saucepan, add the mushrooms and cook over a high heat for 2 minutes, stirring to prevent burning. Drain the mushrooms. Melt the remaining butter in a small saucepan. Add the flour and mix well. Gradually add the stock, stirring over a medium high heat until the sauce comes to the boil and is thick and smooth. Remove from the heat and beat in the mayonnaise. Add the queens, mushrooms and thyme, season with salt and pepper, mix well and transfer at once to four hot, lightly buttered ramekin dishes. Serve at once.

Pilaf with Monk Fish or Huss and Ham

A simple and aromatic rice dish, this is quickly prepared.

Serves 4

1 medium onion
1 fresh chilli
1 green pepper
1 227-g (8-oz) tin tomatoes

113 g (4 oz) cooked ham
6 spring onions
340 g (12 oz) monk fish or huss
Court bouillon (see page 66)
42 g (1½ oz) butter
1 tablespoon olive or vegetable oil
2 tablespoons finely chopped parsley
170 g (6 oz) long-grain rice
Salt and freshly ground black pepper
170 g (6 oz) frozen prawns

Peel and finely chop the onion. Remove the seeds from the chilli and very finely chop the flesh. Remove the core and seeds from the green pepper and finely chop the flesh. Chop the tomatoes; cut the ham into small dice or strips; wash and trim the spring onions and cut each one into thin strips. Cut the fish into bite-sized pieces. Cover with cold *court bouillon*, bring gently to the boil and simmer for about 10–15 minutes until just tender.

Heat the butter with the oil, add the onion, chilli and pepper and cook over a low heat until the vegetables are soft and the onion is transparent. Add the tomatoes and parsley and bring to the boil. Add the rice, stirring well until it becomes transparent. Add enough water to cover the ingredients by about 13 mm (½ in), season, mix well and bring to the boil. Mix in the frozen prawns and ham, cover tightly and cook over a low heat for 20 minutes by which time the rice should be tender and the liquid absorbed.

Turn the pilaf on to a heated serving dish and garnish with thin strips of spring onion. Serve the pilaf with one of the tomato or Espagnole sauce variations. (see pages 223, 225).

Huss with Leeks, Onions and Apples

This delicious fish dish has overtones of Normandy cuisine, and can be served as a starter or a main course.

Serves 4–6

2 large onions
2 leeks
2 cooking apples
450 g (1 lb) huss
57 g (2 oz) butter (a little extra if required)
142 ml ($\frac{1}{4}$ pint) cream
3 tablespoons calvados or chambéry
Salt and freshly ground black pepper

Peel and very thinly slice the onions and divide the slices into rings, discarding the central core. Wash the leeks, trim off any coarse green leaves and cut the leeks into 25-mm (1-in) thick slices. Peel, core and slice the apples and put them into cold salted water until needed to prevent them turning brown. Cut any bones, especially the backbone, from the huss and cut the flesh into 25-mm (1-in) wide strips.

Melt the butter in a large, heavy frying pan. Add the onions and leeks and cook over a low heat, stirring every now and then to prevent sticking, until the onions are soft and transparent.

Remove the onions and leeks with a slotted spoon (leave as much of the juice as possible in the pan) and arrange on a heated serving dish, spreading them out evenly over the bottom.

Drain the apple slices, add to the juices in the frying pan, cover with a lid and cook over a low heat, shaking to prevent sticking or burning, until just soft. Remove and arrange over the onions and leeks.

Add the pieces of fish to the juices in the pan (you may have to add a little more butter) and cook over a medium heat, stirring gently now and then, for about 8 minutes or until the fish is just cooked through. Lower the heat, add the cream and calvados or chambéry, season and stir lightly until the sauce is hot through.

Spoon the fish and sauce over the apples and serve as soon as possible. If liked, garnish with finely chopped parsley or triangles of crisply fried bread.

Pollock Steaks with Greek Sauce

In the summer this dish can be made in advance, chilled overnight and served cold with a salad.

Serves 4

2 large onions
1 stalk celery
450 g (1 lb) ripe tomatoes
1 teaspoon lemon juice
4 pollock or other white fish steaks
5 tablespoons olive or vegetable oil
1 tablespoon tomato purée
142 ml ($\frac{1}{4}$ pint) water or dry white wine
Pinch sugar
1 teaspoon finely chopped fresh dill
Salt and freshly ground black pepper

Peel and chop the onions; thinly slice the celery. Skin and roughly chop the tomatoes. Sprinkle the lemon juice over the fish.

Heat the oil in a saucepan. Add the onions, and cook over a low heat, stirring every now and then, until soft and transparent. Add the tomatoes, tomato puree, celery, water or wine, sugar and the dill and season. Bring to the boil, cover and simmer for 15 minutes, stirring every now and then to prevent sticking.

Transfer the sauce to a shallow frying pan, add the fish and cook over a low heat, uncovered, until the fish is tender and the sauce thick and rich (about 10–15 minutes depending on the thickness of the fish).

Remove the fish on to a warm serving dish and spoon the sauce over.

Creamed Skate with Mushrooms in a Vol-au-Vent Case

If you don't want the bother of making a vol-au-vent case you can often find them in a good baker's shop. Instead of one large case you could use six smaller cases for this recipe, which can also be made with other cooked white fish.

Serves 6

1.1 kg (2½ lb) skate wings
Court bouillon (see page 66)
170 g (6 oz) small, very firm button mushrooms
1 small clove garlic
57 g (2 oz) butter
2 tablespoons flour
285 ml (½ pint) milk
57 g (2 oz) grated Gruyère cheese
142 ml (¼ pint) single cream
Salt and freshly ground black pepper
1 large or 6 small vol-au-vent cases, baked

Place the skate wings in a shallow pan. Cover with cold *court bouillon*, bring slowly to the boil and simmer gently for about 10–15 minutes until the flesh turns opaque and will just flake from the bones. Take out and leave to cool. Remove the flesh from the bones, roughly flaking it into the characteristic shreds.

Slice the mushrooms. Peel and slice the garlic very thinly. Melt the butter, add the mushrooms and garlic and cook over a high heat, stirring, for 2 minutes. Add the flour and mix well. Gradually add the milk and stir continually over a medium heat until the sauce comes to the boil and is thick and smooth. Add the cheese and cook over a low heat, stirring, until it has melted. Lower the heat and stir in the cream. Season and fold in the skate.

Fill the vol-au-vent case or cases with the sauce and heat through in a moderately hot oven (190 °C (375 °F), Reg. 5) for about 5 minutes until hot through.

Whole Fish with Cream and Horseradish Sauce

So much goodness is lost by filleting a fish instead of serving it whole. This is a delicious way of cooking a whole fish and you can use it to cook a red fish, bream, bass or grey mullet – choose whatever is least expensive.

Serves 4

900 g–1.1 kg (2–2$\frac{1}{2}$ lb) fish, cleaned and scaled
1 large onion
1 carrot
1 stalk celery
1 bay leaf
$\frac{1}{2}$ teaspoon salt and freshly ground black pepper
28 g (1 oz) butter
1 tablespoon flour
142 ml ($\frac{1}{4}$ pint) single cream
2 tablespoons finely grated fresh horseradish (or use
   2$\frac{1}{2}$ tablespoons made horseradish sauce)
$\frac{1}{2}$ teaspoon castor sugar
1 teaspoon lemon juice

Peel and slice the onion; wash and roughly chop the carrot; wash and roughly chop the celery. Place in a saucepan with the bay leaf. Season and cover with water. Bring to the boil, cover and simmer for 30 minutes. Remove the bay leaf and strain the stock into a large shallow pan, reserving the vegetables. When the stock is hot, but not boiling, add the fish, cover and cook over a low heat until just tender. Lift out carefully and transfer to a heated serving dish. Spread the cooked vegetables on top and keep warm while making the sauce.

Melt the butter in a small heavy saucepan. Add the flour and mix well. Gradually blend in 142 g ($\frac{1}{4}$ pint) of the fish stock, stirring continually until the sauce comes to the boil and is thick and smooth. Add the cream, horseradish, sugar and lemon juice and heat gently without boiling, stirring all the time, for 3 minutes. Check the seasoning and pour over the fish and vegetables.

Slices of White Fish with Cream Sauce

Serves 6

900 g (2 lb) coley, eel or white fish fillets with the skin removed
1 large onion
57 g (2 oz) butter
2 bay leaves
Salt and freshly ground black pepper
1–2 tablespoons white wine (optional)
1 tablespoon flour
142 g (5 oz) sour cream

Cut the fish into 13-mm ($\frac{1}{2}$-in) thick slices or finger-sized pieces. Peel and slice the onion and divide it into rings. Heat the butter in a large heavy frying pan. Add the onion and cook over a low heat until soft and transparent. Add the bay leaves and the fish, spread over the bottom of the pan, season and pour in just enough water to cover. Bring to the boil, cover and simmer slowly for about 15 minutes until the fish is just tender. Remove it with a slotted spoon on to a heated serving dish and keep warm.

Mix the flour to a smooth paste with the cream. Strain the fish stock and add 285 ml ($\frac{1}{2}$ pint) of it to the cream mixture. Transfer to a saucepan and cook over a low heat until the sauce thickens and comes to a low boil; it should be smooth and shining. Taste for seasoning and pour the finished sauce over the fish.

Note: 1–2 tablespoons of white wine can be added to the fish with the water.

Pollock Divana

Instead of pollock you could well use coley for this dish.

Serves 6

1 onion
2 sprigs parsley
1 sprig thyme
1 bay leaf
900 g (2 lb) pollock fillets
142 ml ($\frac{1}{4}$ pint) dry white wine
1 tablespoon white wine vinegar
Salt and white pepper

For the sauce
42 g ($1\frac{1}{2}$ oz) butter
3 tablespoons flour
285 ml ($\frac{1}{2}$ pint) cooking liquor
142 ml ($\frac{1}{4}$ pint) single cream
28 g (1 oz) finely grated Cheddar cheese
2 teaspoons Parmesan cheese
1 egg yolk, beaten
1 tablespoon finely chopped parsley

Peel and slice the onion and divide into rings. Place the onion, parsley, thyme and bay leaf in a shallow pan, place the fish on top, skin side up, and pour over the white wine and vinegar. Season and add enough cold water to cover the fish. Cover the pan with a lid and leave to stand in a cold place for 2 hours. Bring slowly to the boil and simmer for 15 minutes until the fish is just tender. Skin the fillets and remove them carefully on to a heated serving dish. Keep warm while making the sauce.

Melt two-thirds of the butter in a small saucepan. Add the flour and stir well. Gradually add the fish liquor and cream, stirring continually over a medium heat until the sauce comes to the boil and is thick and smooth. Add the cheese, season and beat in the egg yolk, cooking over a low heat until the sauce is thick and shining and all the cheese has melted. Pour the sauce over the fish, dot with the remaining butter and put under a hot grill until the top is golden brown and bubbling. Sprinkle with finely chopped parsley and serve at once.

Poached Fillets of White Fish Normande

This is classically a way of cooking sole or perhaps plaice but there is no reason why it should not be adapted successfully to other fish. I have done it with coley and it was very acceptable; but best of all were John Dory fillets, with megrim sole and fillets of dab coming a good second best. You could also try making it with fillets of sea bass. The secret, as always, is not to overcook the fish.

Serves 4

4 medium John Dory, megrim sole or large dabs, filleted
Bouquet garni
2 bay leaves
1 onion
2 sticks celery
Salt and freshly ground black pepper
2 shallots
142 ml ($\frac{1}{4}$ pint) dry white wine
113 g (4 oz) fresh, firm button mushrooms
42 g ($1\frac{1}{2}$ oz) butter
285 ml ($\frac{1}{2}$ pint) single cream
Juice of 1 lemon
113 g (4 oz) peeled prawns
Croutons of fried bread or puff pastry

Place the fish fillets in a shallow pan with the bones and skin, bouquet garni, bay leaves, the onion, peeled and sliced and the celery, roughly chopped. Pour over just enough water to cover and season. Bring slowly to the boil, turn down the heat immediately and simmer very gently for about 15 minutes or until the fish is just cooked.

Remove the fillets, strain the cooking liquid and return it to a clean pan. Boil until reduced by half.

Peel and chop the shallots. Put them in a small saucepan, pour over the wine and 142 ml ($\frac{1}{4}$ pint) of the fish liquid, bring to the boil and boil over a high heat until reduced by half. Peel and slice the mushrooms. Heat one-third of the butter, add the mushrooms and cook over a high heat, stirring, for about 2 minutes or until the butter has been absorbed.

Gradually add the cream, lemon juice and remaining butter, cut into small pieces, to the reduced sauce. Stir over a medium heat without boiling. Add the mushrooms and prawns to the sauce and season.

Arrange the cooked fish fillets in a buttered shallow baking dish, pour over the sauce and heat through for about 10 minutes in a moderate oven (180 °C (350 °F), Reg. 4).

Garnish with croutons of fried bread or puff pastry.

Skate Wings with Orange Butter Sauce

The taste of orange goes well with white fish of all kinds and is especially good with skate wings. This is a light and very special fish dish which you could serve as a first course for a dinner party or a main course with rice or a salad. The sauce also goes well with poached fillets of whiting or other white fish.

Serves 4 as a main course

2 medium-sized skate wings
Court bouillon (see page 66)
225 g (8 oz) long-grain rice

For the sauce
Coarsely grated rind and juice of one orange
57 g (2 oz) butter
142 ml ($\frac{1}{4}$ pint) cream
2 egg yolks
Salt and freshly ground black pepper
2 tablespoons finely chopped parsley

Cover the wings with cold *court bouillon*, bring gently to the boil and simmer slowly for about 15 minutes or until the flesh is tender. Remove the wings from the *court bouillon*, leave until cool enough to handle, then remove the dark skin and slide the flesh from the bones.

Place the rice in a saucepan, add a pinch of salt and enough water to come about 19 mm ($\frac{3}{4}$ in) over the rice and bring to the boil. Stir, cover tightly and simmer for about 20 minutes until all the water has been absorbed and the rice is tender. Stir well with a fork and place a ring of rice around a lightly buttered serving dish.

Blanch the orange rind in boiling water for 5 minutes and drain well. Melt the butter in a saucepan, add the cream and bring to the boil. Beat the egg yolks until smooth. Add the butter and cream mixture and beat until smooth. Return to the pan and cook over a low heat, without boiling, until the sauce is thick and the consistency of custard. Add the orange juice and rind, season and add the skate. Heat through, stirring as little as possible.

Put the fish and sauce in the centre of the rice ring and serve as soon as possible, sprinkled with parsley.

Grilled fish

*Some of the best dishes in the world are the simplest
to prepare and cook. Grilled fish falls in this category.
Fish, fresh as can be, quickly cleaned and then swiftly
grilled under a hot flame or over charcoal embers, brushed
with butter or oil and seasoned with salt, pepper and
fresh herbs, is almost unbeatable. But the fish must be
really fresh and of the very best quality.*

Grilled Red Mullet

No book of this kind would be complete without a recipe
for this most delicious of all fish dishes, which I find at its
best served with boiled new potatoes and a crisp salad.

Serves 4

4 medium-sized red mullet
4 tablespoons olive or sunflower oil
Salt
Lemon wedges

Clean the fish but leave the liver in place. Remove the gills.
Cut two slashes in each side of the fish, diagonally through
the skin to the bone and salt lightly. Brush the fish with oil
and grill them under a fairly fierce heat for about 7 minutes
on each side until the skin is crisp and golden (it can even
be slightly burnt) and the flesh cooked through. Serve
immediately with the juices from the pan poured over,
garnished with a juicy wedge of lemon.

Curried Fish Kebabs

Serve these with rice and the usual curry accompaniments.

Serves 4

900 g (2 lb) filleted white fish (coley, bass, bream, etc.,
    or best of all monk fish or huss)
Juice of $\frac{1}{2}$ lemon
1 teaspoon ground cumin
$\frac{1}{2}$ teaspoon chilli powder

1 teaspoon garam masala or curry powder
285 ml ($\frac{1}{2}$ pint) yoghurt
Salt
2 onions
Oil

Cut the fish into 38-mm ($1\frac{1}{2}$-in) pieces. Place in a bowl and sprinkle with the lemon juice. Mix well so that all the fish is flavoured.

Add the cumin, chilli powder and garam masala or curry powder to the yoghurt and mix well; season with a little salt. Pour the yoghurt paste over the fish, mix well, cover and refrigerate for at least 1 hour before using.

Peel and slice the onion. Put the fish on to skewers with a slice of onion in between each piece, brush with oil and grill under a moderate heat, turning frequently and basting with some of the yoghurt mixture and a little more oil if the kebabs get too brown.

Barbecued Mackerel

Serves 4

3 small mackerel
1 clove garlic
142 ml ($\frac{1}{4}$ pint) olive or sunflower oil
3 tablespoons lemon juice
1 teaspoon salt
Freshly ground black pepper
2 tablespoons finely chopped parsley
Tomato sauce (see page 222)

Clean the mackerel, leaving on their heads and tails but removing the gills. Cut slashes through the skin on both sides at 50-mm (2-in) intervals. Peel and crush the garlic. Place the mackerel in a shallow dish and rub the garlic into the slashes.

Combine the oil and lemon juice, season and mix in the

parsley. Pour the marinade over the mackerel and leave to marinate for 1 hour, turning from time to time.

Grill the fish over hot charcoal (or under a hot grill), brushing from time to time with the marinade. They will probably need about 6 minutes on each side. Serve with baked jacket potatoes, green salad and tomato sauce.

Sea Bass with Olive Sauce

Serves 4–6

2 bass weighing about 675 g (1½ lb) each
Flour
Salt and freshly ground black pepper
2 spring onions
1 clove garlic
1 red pepper
57 g (2 oz) black olives
113 g (4 oz) stuffed green olives
7 tablespoons oil
2 tablespoons finely chopped parsley
1 tablespoon capers, chopped
142 ml (¼ pint) dry white wine
2 teaspoons tomato purée
28 g (1 oz) butter
4 tablespoons fresh white breadcrumbs

Clean the fish, remove the heads and tails and cut each fish into four. Wash the pieces and dry well on kitchen paper. Season some flour and coat the fish pieces with it.

Peel and finely chop the spring onions. Peel and crush the garlic. Remove the core and seeds of the red pepper and cut the pepper into thin strips. Remove the stones from the black olives and finely chop, with the green olives. Heat 4 tablespoons of the oil, add the spring onions, garlic and red pepper and cook over a low heat until the onion is soft and transparent. Add the parsley, capers and olives and continue to cook gently for a further 5 minutes, stirring to prevent sticking. Add the wine and tomato purée and simmer for 5 minutes.

Heat the remaining oil with the butter in a shallow frying pan. Add the fish and cook over a low heat until it is browned on both sides (about 6 minutes each side). Pour over the sauce and simmer for a further 3 minutes. Place the fish on a heated serving dish, cover with the sauce, sprinkle with breadcrumbs and brown under a hot grill for just a couple of minutes.

Grilled Fillets of Mackerel with Fennel

This is a classic way of serving red mullet but is also very good indeed made with fillets of less expensive mackerel or sea bass. You need the bulbous roots of the Florentine fennel for the dish; these can be found at most good green-grocer's. If you can't get fennel substitute a ratatouille or just serve the grilled, mustard-flavoured mackerel by themselves.

Serves 6

3 fennel bulbs
1 large onion
57 g (2 oz) butter
6 large mackerel fillets
1 tablespoon olive or sunflower oil
1 tablespoon Dijon mustard
Salt and freshly ground black pepper

Remove the green tops and hard base of the fennel bulbs and thickly slice the flesh in the same way that you would an onion. Peel and thinly slice the onion and divide it into rings.

Blanch the sliced fennel in boiling salted water for 10 minutes and drain well.

Melt the butter in a frying pan. Add the onion and fennel and cook over a low heat, stirring to prevent sticking, until the onion is soft and both vegetables are cooked through. Transfer to a warm serving dish and keep warm.

Cut slashes at 25-mm (1-in) intervals through the skin of the mackerel fillets. Combine the oil and mustard, season and rub into the skin of the mackerel. Put the mackerel under a hot grill for about 8 minutes or until they are cooked through and the skins are crisp and slightly scorched. Place on top of the fennel and onion mixture and serve at once.

Coley en Brochette

The firm flesh of the coley makes it an excellent subject for cooking as kebabs, but you can use any other firm-fleshed fish – monk fish, if you can get it, is probably best of all.

Serves 4

675 g ($1\frac{1}{2}$ lb) firm white fish
142 ml ($\frac{1}{4}$ pint) olive or sunflower oil
Juice of 1 lemon
2 bay leaves
Pinch dried mixed herbs
1 teaspoon grated onion
Salt and freshly ground black pepper
1 large onion
8 small tomatoes

Cut the fish into 38-mm ($1\frac{1}{2}$-in) squares and place them in a dish. Combine the oil, lemon juice, bay leaves, mixed herbs and grated onion; season well. Pour this mixture over the fish, and leave to marinate for at least half an hour.

Cut the outer layers of the onion into squares the same size as the fish.

Put a tomato at the end of each skewer and thread on the fish pieces with a piece of onion between each. Baste the kebabs well with the marinating liquid and grill them under a fairly fierce heat, turning frequently and basting every now and then with the pan juices. This should take about 8 minutes.

Arrange the skewers on a bed of saffron-flavoured or savoury rice and serve with a salad.

Fish Florentine

This is a good dish to serve when you are slimming. Fish has virtually no fat content and is therefore a very good slimming ingredient.

Serves 4

675 g (1½ lb) spinach
Juice of ½ lemon
Salt, pepper and a little ground nutmeg
42 g (1½ oz) butter
4 fish fillets (mackerel, bass, bream, grey mullet or any other firm-fleshed fish)
4 eggs

Cook the spinach in a little boiling salted water until it is tender; drain well. Mix in the lemon juice and season with salt, pepper and a little nutmeg. Arrange the spinach in the bottom of a buttered serving dish and keep warm.

Melt the butter. Arrange the fish fillets on a grill rack, brush with melted butter and season. Grill the fish for about 6–8 minutes until cooked.

While the fish is grilling poach the eggs lightly. Drain and keep warm until the fish is cooked. Arrange the fish on the spinach, top with the eggs and serve at once.

Variations

For a more substantial dish cover with a rich cheese sauce, sprinkle over a little extra cheese and brown under a hot grill.

Perch with Poached Egg and Cream Sauce

This is a good dish to make with really fresh fillets of perch.

Serves 4

4 perch, filleted
Juice of ½ lemon
Salt and white pepper
85 g (3 oz) butter
1½ tablespoons flour
Scant 285 ml (½ pint) milk
142 ml (¼ pint) sour cream
4 eggs
½ teaspoon paprika

Place the fillets on a grill rack, brush with lemon juice and season.

Melt half the butter in a saucepan, add the flour and mix well. Gradually add the milk, stirring continually over a medium high heat until the sauce comes to the boil and is thick and smooth. Simmer for 3 minutes, then stir in the sour cream and season.

Poach the eggs until just set and drain them.

Melt the remaining butter, dribble it over the fish and grill them under a medium high heat until just cooked. Divide the fillets into pairs and arrange them on a heated serving dish.

Place a poached egg on top of each pair, pour over the sauce and sprinkle with the paprika.

Fish Fillets with Crispy Cheese Topping

Use any good quality fish for this simple but delicious dish. I have had great success with fillets of pollock, bream, bass, coley and monk fish, and it is also an extremely good way to cook mackerel.

Serves 4

675 g (1½ lb) fish fillets, skin removed
Juice ½ lemon
Salt and freshly ground black pepper
57 g (2 oz) freshly grated brown breadcrumbs
57 g (2 oz) finely grated Cheddar cheese
1 tablespoon cream
1 tablespoon sunflower oil

Lightly oil a shallow baking dish. Place the fillets in the dish, sprinkle them with lemon juice and season.

Combine the breadcrumbs with the grated cheese and mix well. Mix in the cream and spread the mixture over the fillets. Dribble over the oil and grill the fish under a medium hot flame (keep the fillets to within about 13 mm (½ in) of the flame) until the topping is brown and the fish cooked.

Variation

Grill the fillets on a base of aubergines and tomatoes and you will have an unusual and substantial dish.

225 g (½ lb) aubergines
1 small onion
1 clove garlic
1 227-g (8-oz) tin tomatoes
2 tablespoons vegetable oil
Salt and freshly ground black pepper
Pinch thyme, oregano and basil

Cut the aubergines into small dice. Peel and finely chop the onion; peel and crush the garlic. Chop the tomatoes, reserving the juice.

Heat the oil, add the onion and garlic and cook over a low heat until the onion is soft and transparent. Add the aubergine and continue cooking until it is soft and most of the oil has been absorbed. Add the tomatoes, season, mix in the herbs, bring to the boil and simmer gently for 30 minutes. Spread the aubergine mixture over the bottom of a lightly oiled baking dish, top with the fish and continue as above.

Barbecued Whiting

Try this way of cooking whiting, eat it out of doors, preferably with a glass of rough red wine (yes, red – cheap red is much better than cheap white) and you will never underrate this fish again.

Serves 4

2 whiting (large ones weighing about 675–900 g
   (1½–2 lb))
Salt and freshly ground black pepper
Olive or sunflower oil
8 bay leaves

Clean the whiting and discard the head and tail. Cut each fish diagonally into four pieces. Rub with salt and pepper and brush with oil. Spear two pieces of fish on to each of four skewers, with 2 bay leaves in between. Cook them about 100 mm (4 in) above dying charcoal, basting every now and then with more oil if the fish looks dry. Turn frequently and allow about 10 minutes cooking time.

Stuffed Mackerel

Serves 4

4 small mackerel
2 onions
2 teaspoons mustard powder
8 tablespoons crushed porridge oats
Salt and freshly ground black pepper
4 tablespoons sunflower oil

Clean and wash the fish and remove the heads and tails. Score through the flesh to the bone at 25-mm (1-in) intervals on both sides. Peel and coarsely grate the onions. Combine with the mustard and crushed oats and season.

Fill the cavity of the mackerel with this stuffing and spread any remaining in the scores on both sides. Brush the fish with the oil and grill under a low heat for 8 minutes on each side until cooked through.

Serve with boiled rice and a green or mixed salad, or vegetables in season.

Fillets of Bass with Orange and Dubonnet Sauce

Few dishes can be better than grilled bass straight from the sea.

Serves 4

2 sea bass weighing about 900 g (2 lb) each
Salt and freshly ground black pepper
85 g (3 oz) melted butter
Orange and Dubonnet sauce (see page 241)
Finely chopped parsley

Bone the bass into two fillets each. Arrange the fillets on a grill pan, skin side down, and season. Melt the butter, brush the fillets with it and grill under a fairly high heat for about 10 minutes until crisp and cooked through.

Follow the instructions for making the orange sauce on page 241.

Arrange the fish fillets in a lightly greased serving dish, pour over the sauce, sprinkle with parsley and serve at once.

Monk Fish en Brochette

You can make this simple marinaded and grilled dish with any firm-fleshed white fish, but monk fish or huss is particularly suitable. The dish has a delicate flavour and should be served with plain boiled rice and a green or mixed salad.

If you are having a barbecue then the taste of this dish will be even better if it is cooked in the open over charcoal.

Serves 4

900 g (2 lb) monk fish or huss
4 tablespoons sour cream
4 tablespoons lemon juice
Salt and freshly ground black pepper
28 g (1 oz) melted butter
1 bunch spring onions
3 firm tomatoes
1 lemon
3 tablespoons finely chopped parsley

Skin the fish and remove any bones. Cut the fish into neat cubes about 38 mm ($1\frac{1}{2}$ in) square. Combine the sour cream and lemon juice and season. Add the fish and mix well so that the pieces are all coated. Leave to stand in a cool place for at least 2 hours before cooking.

Thread the fish on eight skewers (see notes on cooking fish en brochette on page 58) and cook under a hot grill about 75 mm (3 in) away from the heat for about 10 minutes, basting with the melted butter and any leftover marinade.

Clean the spring onions and cut into four, lengthwise. Cut the tomatoes into eighths and cut the lemon into quarters, removing the pips.

Put the skewered fish on a heated serving dish, garnish with the spring onions, parsley lemon wedges and tomatoes and serve at once.

Curried Monk Fish Kebabs

Serves 4

900 g (2 lb) monk fish
4 tablespoons olive or vegetable oil
1 teaspoon lemon juice

1 teaspoon curry paste
2 green or red peppers
1 large onion
Bay leaves

Cut the monk fish into 25-mm (1-in) cubes. Combine the oil, lemon juice and curry paste, mix well, add the monk fish cubes and leave to marinate for 1 hour.

Remove the seeds and core of the peppers and cut the flesh into 1-in-square pieces. Peel the onion, separate the layers and cut them into 25-mm (1-in) square pieces. Blanch the pieces of pepper and onion in boiling water for 3 minutes and drain well.

Skewer the pieces of monk fish, interspersing them with onion, pepper and bay leaves. Brush with the remaining marinade and cook under a hot grill for about 15 minutes, turning every now and then. Serve at once on a bed of rice.

Huss in a Rich Sauce

This is another dish which can be served as either a first or a main course. It is on the rich side, so precede or follow it with something light. Serve it as a main course with mashed potatoes or rice and a green or mixed salad.

Serves 4–6

1 large onion
450 g (1 lb) huss
1 tablespoon oil
28 g (1 oz) butter
2 tablespoons flour
285 ml ($\frac{1}{2}$ pint) milk
4 tablespoons home-made tomato purée (see page 223)
1$\frac{1}{2}$ teaspoons paprika
1 tablespoon medium sherry
28 g (1 oz) finely grated Parmesan cheese
Salt and freshly ground black pepper

Few drops Tabasco sauce
1 egg yolk
3 tablespoons double cream
Fresh white breadcrumbs

Peel and chop the onion. Remove any bone from the huss and cut the fish into 25-mm (1-in) wide strips.

Heat the oil and half the butter in a heavy saucepan. Add the onion and cook over a low heat, stirring to prevent sticking, until soft and transparent. Mix in the flour and stir well. Gradually blend in the milk, stirring continually over a medium high heat, until the mixture is smooth and free from lumps. Add the tomato purée, paprika, sherry and half the Parmesan and cook over a medium heat until the sauce is bubbling and the cheese has melted. Season with salt, pepper and a few drops of Tabasco. Add the pieces of fish and simmer gently for about 8 minutes or until just tender.

Beat the egg yolk with the cream until the mixture is smooth, add to the fish and stir gently over a low heat for 2 minutes without boiling. Transfer the mixture to a fireproof serving dish and sprinkle the breadcrumbs and remaining cheese over the surface. Dot with the remaining butter cut into very small pieces and brown under a hot grill.

Baked fish

*You can bake almost any fish and come up with a good
dish providing that the fish is not allowed to dry out
during the cooking time or to overcook. There are so many
different recipes and so many different ways of baking fish that
my only advice, outside the recipes contained in this book, is
to trust your own judgment and ring the changes by using
your imagination and the fish you have available.*

Baked Whole Fish with Onions and Bacon

Try this with whiting, grey mullet or any other white-fleshed fish.

Serves 4

1 large onion
1 small fennel root
85 g (3 oz) thinly cut streaky bacon rashers
1 whole white fish weighing about 900 g (2 lb)
3 tablespoons oil
2 tablespoons dry white wine
Salt and freshly ground black pepper

For the sauce
1½ tablespoons flour
285 ml (½ pint) chicken stock
1 teaspoon made English mustard
2 tablespoons finely chopped parsley

Well oil a baking dish. Peel and thinly slice the onion; thinly slice the fennel root; remove the bacon rinds. Arrange the fish in the baking dish, surround with the onions and fennel and cover with the bacon. Pour over the oil and wine and season well.

Bake in a moderate oven (190 °C (375 °F), Reg. 5) for about 30 minutes, basting with the juices in the pan every now and then, until the fish is just tender. Transfer the fish to a heated serving dish.

Place the baking pan over a low heat and blend in the flour until all the flour lumps disappear. Gradually beat in the stock, stirring continually, until the sauce comes to the boil and thickens. Mix in the mustard and parsley and check the seasoning.

Serve the fish with boiled potatoes, a green vegetable and the sauce on the side.

Variation

Prepare a tomato sauce (see page 222) and bake the fish in it.

Bacon-Stuffed Mackerel

I invented this dish when Julie (my right hand in the kitchen) produced a bucketful of mackerel in the kitchen one evening. They had quite literally fallen off the back of a lorry – it had overturned and lost its load.

Serves 4

4 medium-sized mackerel
1 small onion
113 g (4 oz) streaky bacon
Salt and freshly ground black pepper
Pinch of dried sage

Clean the mackerel and remove their heads and tails. Cut diagonal slashes in the sides, through to the bones. Peel the onion.

Mince the bacon with the onion through the fine blades of a mincing machine. Season the mixture with salt (unless the bacon is very salty) and pepper and mix in a pinch of sage. Press the mixture into the slashes in the side of the mackerel.

Arrange the mackerel in a greased baking dish and bake in a moderate oven (190 °C (375 °F), Reg. 5) for about 30 minutes.

Serve with new or mashed potatoes and cabbage.

Mackerel with Gooseberry and Lemon Stuffing

Serves 4

4 medium mackerel, filleted
225 g (8 oz) goosebcrries
57 g (2 oz) butter
4 tablespoons fresh white breadcrumbs
Grated rind of $\frac{1}{2}$ lemon
1 teaspoon lemon juice
Salt, freshly ground black pepper and a pinch of
  cayenne

Combine the gooseberries (tops and tails removed) in a saucepan with the butter. Cook over a very low heat until soft, then mash with a wooden spoon or purée them in liquidiser. Leave to cool. Add the breadcrumbs, lemon rind and juice and season with salt, pepper and cayenne.

Arrange four fillets, skin-side down, in a well-buttered baking dish, spread over the gooseberry mixture and top with the remaining fillets, skin-side up. Cover with a piece of buttered greaseproof paper and bake in a moderate oven (190 °C (375 °F), Reg. 5) for 30 minutes.

Barquettes of Bass

These light little mouthfuls of well-flavoured fish in pastry can be served as a first course, with drinks or as an accompaniment to soup. I make mine from bass but you could easily substitute coley, pollock or any other fairly firm-fleshed white fish.

Serves 4 as a first course
225 g (8 oz) puff pastry
1 egg

285 ml ($\frac{1}{2}$ pint) white sauce (see page 212)
225 g (8 oz) cooked white fish
28 g (1 oz) grated Cheddar cheese
Salt and freshly ground black pepper
$\frac{1}{2}$ teaspoon anchovy essence
Pinch nutmeg or mace

Roll the pastry out thinly and use half to line boat-shaped cases (barquettes). Beat the egg into the white sauce. Flake the fish, add it to the white sauce with the cheese, season and flavour with a little anchovy essence and a pinch of nutmeg or mace. Leave to cool and then half fill the barquettes with the mixture.

Roll out the remaining pastry thinly and cut tops for the barquettes. Press edges firmly together, cut an air vent in the top, brush with a little milk and bake in a hot oven (220 °C (425 °F), Reg. 7) for 15 minutes.

Serve the barquettes hot, warm or cold.

Bass Stuffed with Walnuts

Serves 4

2 bass about 675–900 g ($1\frac{1}{2}$–2 lb) each
Salt and freshly ground black pepper
1 bread roll
Milk
170 g (6 oz) shelled walnuts
2 eggs, separated
Pinch of dried sage
57 g (2 oz) butter

Clean the fish, rub it with salt and leave it to stand for 5 minutes.

Break up the bread roll and soak it in milk until soft. Squeeze out excess milk. Mince the walnuts through the coarse blades of a mincing machine.

Combine the bread, egg yolks and walnuts, season and

mix in the sage. Whip the egg whites until stiff and fold them into the stuffing. Stuff the bass with this mixture, place them in a greased baking dish and dot with butter. Bake in a moderate oven (190 °C (375 °F), Reg. 5) for about 30 minutes or until just cooked through.

Serve the fish hot with one of the more robust sauces or with a seasoned butter.

Mackerel with Cider and Onion

Some recipes use raw onions but I find it is essential to cook them first.

Serves 4

3 onions
57 g (2 oz) butter
1½ tablespoons white wine vinegar
Salt and freshly ground black pepper
4 large or 8 small fillets mackerel
4 tablespoons dry white breadcrumbs
142 ml (¼ pint) dry cider
142 ml (¼ pint) double cream

Peel and thinly slice the onions and divide into rings. Melt three-quarters of the butter in a frying pan, add the onions and cook over a low heat, stirring to prevent sticking, for about 10 minutes until really soft. Add the vinegar and continue to cook for a further 5 minutes. Season well.

Arrange the mackerel in a shallow, well-oiled baking dish and cover with the onions. Sprinkle with the breadcrumbs and pour over the cider. Bake in a moderate oven (190 °C (375 °F), Reg. 5) for about 25 minutes.

Pour over the cream and put the dish under a hot grill until the top is bubbling and golden. Serve with boiled potatoes and a green vegetable or salad.

Coley with Mushrooms and Cider

Serves 4

900 g (2 lb) coley
1 medium onion
113 g (4 oz) firm button mushrooms
28 g (1 oz) butter
2 tablespoons flour
Salt and freshly ground black pepper
1 tablespoon olive oil
570 ml (1 pint) dry cider
1 tablespoon finely chopped parsley

Divide the coley into serving portions and arrange them in an oiled baking dish. Peel and finely chop the onion. Chop the mushrooms. Melt the butter, add the flour and mix well. Remove from the heat, mix in the chopped onions and mushrooms and season. Spread the mixture thinly over the fish fillets. Sprinkle with parsley.

Combine the oil and cider and pour it over the fish. Bake, uncovered, in a moderate oven (180 °C (350 °F), Reg. 4) for about 30 minutes, basting with the juices in the pan after 15 minutes.

Serve with mashed potatoes and a green vegetable.

Stuffed and Baked Conger Eel

Serves 6

1.4 kg (3 lb) conger eel cut from the head end
1 onion
2 tablespoons white wine vinegar
3 tablespoons oil
Salt and freshly ground black pepper
2 bay leaves
2 anchovy fillets
3 tablespoons fresh white breadcrumbs

1 tablespoon finely chopped parsley
Grated rind of $\frac{1}{2}$ lemon
Pinch of dried mixed herbs
Anchovy essence
14 g ($\frac{1}{2}$ oz) melted butter
Milk
Seasoned flour
57 g (2 oz) butter

Wash the eel in salted water, rinse well and remove any fins. Peel and chop the onion. Add the onion to the vinegar and oil and season. Add the bay leaves, pour the marinade over the eel and leave it in a cool place for 4 hours turning every now and then.

Finely chop the anchovy fillets. Combine the bread-crumbs, parsley, lemon rind and herbs and mix in a little anchovy essence and the melted butter. Season and add enough milk to make a stiff stuffing.

Drain off the marinade from the eel (this marinade cannot be used again) and cut the eel through to the bone on both sides at 100-mm (4-in) intervals. Spread the stuffing in these cuts, dredge the eel in seasoned flour and place it on a large sheet of foil. Melt the butter, pour it over the eel and roll up neatly in the foil to keep the stuffing in place.

Bake the eel in a moderate oven (190 °C (375 °F), Reg. 5) for $1\frac{1}{2}$ hours, opening up the foil for the last 10 minutes of cooking time.

To serve, unwrap the eel, sprinkle with a little more chopped parsley and accompany with any of the white sauces on pages 212–215.

Welsh Conger Eel Pie

The rather strong flavour of conger eel makes it a good subject for fish pies.

Serves 6

4 leeks
2 cloves garlic
1 onion
450 g (1 lb) tomatoes
3 tablespoons sunflower oil
Freshly ground black pepper
3 anchovy fillets
2 teaspoons tomato purée
675 g (1½ lb) conger eel
57 g (2 oz) butter
1½ tablespoons flour
425 ml (¾ pint) milk
675 g (1½ lb) potatoes
Salt, pepper and a pinch nutmeg
2 tablespoons cream
42 g (1½ oz) grated Cheddar cheese
Cayenne pepper
Court bouillon (see page 66)

Clean the leeks and cut them into slices about 25 mm (1 in) thick. Peel and crush the garlic. Peel and chop the onion. Scald the tomatoes, slide off skins, remove the core and seeds and chop the flesh.

Heat the oil, add the garlic, leeks and onion and cook over a low heat, stirring, for 5 minutes. Add the tomatoes, season with pepper and simmer for about 15 minutes, stirring every now and then to prevent sticking, until the leeks are soft. Chop the anchovies, add them to the pan with the tomato purée and simmer for a further 5 minutes.

Cut the conger eel into steaks, place them in a shallow pan, cover them with cold *court bouillon*, bring to the boil and simmer gently for about 20 minutes or until the flesh will flake from the bone. Drain off the liquid and remove the skin and bones from the fish. Very roughly flake the flesh and arrange it in a pie dish.

Melt three-quarters of the butter in a saucepan, add the flour and mix well. Gradually add the milk, stirring continually over a medium high heat until the sauce comes to the boil and is thick and smooth. Add the tomato mixture and mix well. Pour over the conger eel and mix lightly.

Peel, cook and mash the potatoes and season with salt, pepper and a pinch of nutmeg. Beat in the remaining butter and 2 tablespoons cream and spread the potatoes over the pie. Sprinkle over the cheese, dust with a little cayenne and bake in a moderately hot oven (200 °C (400 °F), Reg. 6) until the pie is hot through and the potatoes are golden brown.

Gigot of Monk Fish

In France the tail of the monk fish (the bit sold in the fishmonger's) is often referred to as a *gigot* because its shape rather resembles that of a leg of lamb. Dipped in beaten egg, covered with seasoned breadcrumbs and roasted, the *gigot* make delicious eating. You need small tails and should serve them with a tomato sauce poured over.

Serves 4

4 monk fish tails of about 225 g (8 oz) each (or use 1
   large piece if the small ones are not available)
1 egg, beaten
Dried white breadcrumbs
Salt and freshly ground black pepper
6 tablespoons olive or sunflower oil
Juice of 1 lemon
Tomato sauce (see page 222)

Dip the tails in beaten egg and coat them in seasoned breadcrumbs. Arrange the tails in a roasting pan and pour the oil and lemon juice over. Cook them in a moderately hot oven (200 °C (400 °F), Reg. 6) for about 30 minutes, basting frequently, until the fish is cooked through and the outside crisp and golden brown.

Fish Pasties

Serves 6

340 g (¾ lb) puff pastry
85 g (3 oz) ham
2 hard-boiled eggs
1 onion
14 g (½ oz) butter
225 g (½ lb) cooked white fish (coley, red fish, carp, etc.)
142 ml (¼ pint) white sauce (see page 212)
Salt and freshly ground black pepper
Pinch cayenne
Pinch mixed herbs or 1 tablespoon finely chopped parsley
Grated rind of ½ lemon
1 small egg, beaten

Roll out the pastry thinly and cut into six 175-mm (7-in) circles. Mince the ham. Very finely chop the hard-boiled eggs. Peel and finely chop the onion.

Melt the butter, add the chopped onion and cook over a low heat until the onion is soft and transparent. Add the onions, fish, ham and hard-boiled egg to the white sauce and season with salt, pepper and a pinch of cayenne. Mix in the herbs and grated lemon rind.

Divide the filling between the six pastry circles. Brush the edges with beaten egg and pull up over the filling. Crimp firmly together, brush the pastry with beaten egg and bake in a moderately hot oven (200 °C (400 °F), Reg. 6) for about 30 minutes until the pastry is golden brown and puffed.

Coley and Prawn Pie

Coley, with its rich taste and good texture, is an excellent subject for fish pie. This is a fairly standard version, but you can ring the changes *ad infinitum*, adding more or less parsley or other herbs, topping them with mashed, scalloped or Duchesse potatoes or with puff or short crust pastry. You can spike them with Worcestershire sauce, Tabasco or Harvey's sauce, chopped anchovies or anchovy essence. Or add some chopped tomatoes, chopped pimentos or chopped peppers.

Serves 6

450 g (1 lb) coley fillets
225 g (8 oz) smoked haddock
285 ml ($\frac{1}{2}$ pint) milk
2 tablespoons finely chopped parsley
Salt and freshly ground black pepper
1 onion
42 g ($1\frac{1}{2}$ oz) butter
1 tablespoon flour
285 ml ($\frac{1}{2}$ pint) white wine
4 tablespoons double cream
85 g (3 oz) peeled prawns
285 g (10 oz) puff pastry
Beaten egg

Place the coley fillets and smoked haddock in a shallow pan, cover with the milk (you may need to add a little more), add the parsley and season. Bring slowly to the boil and simmer for about 10 minutes until the fish is tender. Drain off the liquid and remove any skin and bones from the fish. Flake the fish.

Peel and very finely chop the onion. Melt the butter in a saucepan, add the onion and cook over a low heat until soft and transparent. Add the flour and mix well. Gradually blend in the milk the fish was cooked in, stirring continually over a medium high heat until the sauce is thick and smooth.

Blend in the wine and the cream; cook for 2 minutes without boiling and season. Add the fish and the prawns and turn into a pie dish.

Roll out the pastry, damp the rim of the pie dish and cover the pie, pressing the pastry down firmly. Brush with beaten egg, cut two air vents and bake the pie in a moderately hot oven (200 °C (400 °F), Reg. 6) for about 30 minutes until the pastry is risen and golden brown.

Pain de Poisson

The only English translation for this dish is Fish Loaf, which does not do justice to the delicious flavouring of this delicate dish. I have made it with coley, sea bass and with fillets of John Dory when they have been plentiful and not too expensive.

Serves 4

28 g (1 oz) butter
2 tablespoons flour
285 ml ($\frac{1}{2}$ pint) milk
340 g ($\frac{3}{4}$ lb) white fish fillets, skin and bones removed
Salt and freshly ground black pepper
170 g (6 oz) peeled prawns
2 eggs
2 egg yolks
198 ml (7 fl oz) double cream
1 tablespoon finely chopped parsley
2 teaspoons finely chopped chives

Make a white sauce by melting the butter, adding the flour and then gradually adding the milk, stirring continually over a medium high heat until the sauce comes to the boil and is thick and smooth. Leave to cool.

Pound the fish with some salt and pepper to a smooth paste in a mortar or reduce it to a fine purée in a liquidiser or food processor. Very finely chop the prawns.

Combine the fish and prawns with the white sauce and

mix well. Beat the eggs and yolks until smooth. Add the cream, beaten eggs, parsley and chives to the fish, mix well and season with a little more salt and pepper (if you want to check the seasoning poach a teaspoon of the mixture in a little boiling water and then taste).

Turn the mixture into a well-buttered loaf tin, place in a baking tin of hot water and cover with buttered greaseproof paper or foil. Bake in a moderate oven (180 °C (350 °F), Reg. 4) for 40 minutes or until a knitting needle plunged into the centre of the fish comes out clean.

Turn the loaf out and serve it with a colourful sauce such as tomato or Espagnole, or a well-flavoured mayonnaise.

Coley in Cider with a Tomato Sauce

Fish, cider and tomatoes go together like the proverbial horse and carriage. Together they delight the palate and tickle the appetite buds. This is a recipe which combines all three in a gloriously simple and quickly made dish.

Serves 4

567 g (1¼ lb) coley fillet
Salt and freshly ground black pepper
1 onion
113 g (4 oz) firm button mushrooms
4 firm, ripe tomatoes
1 stick celery
113 g (4 oz) butter
285 ml (½ pint) dry cider
2 tablespoons finely chopped parsley

Cut the fillets into slices about 75 mm (3 in) square, season and place in a buttered baking dish.

Peel and very thinly slice the onion. Slice the mushrooms. Peel and chop the tomatoes. Very thinly slice the celery.

Melt the butter, add the onion and celery and cook over a low heat until the onion is soft and transparent. Add the mushrooms and tomatoes and continue to cook over a moderate heat for a further 2 minutes. Season and pour the vegetables over the coley fillets. Add the cider, cover with buttered greaseproof paper and bake for 20 minutes in a moderate oven (190 °C (375 °F), Reg. 5). Sprinkle over the chopped parsley and serve at once.

Fish and Mushroom Pie

Serves 6

340 g (12 oz) fish fillets (coley, red fish, whiting, etc., skin removed)
4 anchovy fillets
113 g (4 oz) mushrooms
42 g (1½ oz) butter
1½ tablespoons flour
285 ml (½ pint) milk
Salt and freshly ground black pepper
Pinch chopped dill, fresh or dried
1 tablespoon white wine vinegar
225 g (8 oz) shortcrust or puff pastry
Milk or beaten egg

Cut the fish into bite-sized pieces and arrange in a fairly shallow greased pie dish. Cut the anchovies into small pieces and arrange over the fish. Soak dried dill in vinegar.

Cut the mushrooms into thin slices. Melt the butter in a saucepan, add the mushrooms and toss them over a high heat for 2 minutes. Lower the heat, mix in the flour and gradually blend in the milk, stirring continually over a medium high heat until the sauce comes to the boil and is thick and smooth. Season and mix in the dill. Pour the sauce over the fish and anchovies.

Roll out the pastry, top the pie with the pastry and brush with milk or a small egg, beaten. Bake the pie in a moderately hot oven (200 °C (400 °F), Reg. 6) for 25 minutes.

Baked Fish with Vegetables

The vegetables add a lot of flavour in this dish so that it makes a good way to cook the slightly uninteresting red fish or even those exotic but disappointing carp that one often sees on sale these days.

Serves 6

1 onion
1 green pepper
2 tomatoes
450 g (1 lb) potatoes
2 tablespoons sunflower oil
Salt, pepper and a little paprika
675 g (1½ lb) fish fillets (carp, red fish, whiting, etc.)
285 ml (½ pint) water
285 ml (½ pint) dry white wine
28 g (1 oz) cornflour
142 g (5 oz) sour cream
1 tablespoon finely chopped parsley

Peel and thinly slice the onion and divide into rings. Remove the core and seeds of the pepper and cut the flesh into thin slices. Scald the tomatoes, slide off skins, remove the core and seeds and chop the flesh. Peel and thinly slice the potatoes. Arrange half the potatoes in the bottom of a well-buttered baking dish.

Heat the oil, add the onions and cook over a low heat until soft and transparent. Add the pepper and continue to cook over a low heat for 3 minutes. Add the tomatoes, mix well, season with salt, pepper and paprika and cook for a further 2 minutes, stirring.

Spread half the vegetable mixture over the potatoes, top with the fish and then cover with the remaining vegetable mixture and the rest of the potatoes. Season with a little more salt, pepper and paprika, pour over the water and wine, cover tightly with buttered foil and bake in a moderately hot oven (200 °C (400 °F), Reg. 6) for 30 minutes or until the potatoes are tender. Drain off the cooking liquid, put it in a saucepan, bring it to the boil and boil for 5 minutes until reduced to about half.

Mix the cornflour to a smooth paste with the sour cream. Add the mixture to the fish liquid and cook over a moderate heat, stirring all the time until the sauce is thick and smooth. Add the parsley and pour the sauce over the baked fish dish.

Skate Wings in Cream

This is a very rich dish but one that can be highly recommended.

Serves 4

4 skate wings, skinned
Salt and freshly ground black pepper
Juice of $\frac{1}{2}$ lemon
425 ml ($\frac{3}{4}$ pint) double cream
57 g (2 oz) freshly grated Parmesan cheese

Place the wings in a shallow buttered baking dish. Season and brush with the lemon juice. Pour over the cream, sprinkle with Parmesan cheese and bake in a moderate oven (180 °C (350 °F), Reg. 4) for about 30 minutes or until the fish is just cooked.

Serve with boiled rice and a seasonable vegetable.

Baked Mackerel with Tarragon

Tarragon tends to be thought of as a flavouring for chicken or eggs but it goes extremely well with fish, especially the more oily ones like mackerel. Use fresh tarragon when possible. If you have to use dried tarragon soak it first in a little lemon juice or hot water to bring out the flavour.

Serves 4

4 mackerel
57 g (2 oz) butter
1 teaspoon tarragon, freshly chopped, or use ½ teaspoon
   dried tarragon
1 teaspoon dry mustard
Salt and freshly ground black pepper
142 ml (¼ pint) single cream

Clean the mackerel, remove their heads and tails and arrange them neatly in a buttered baking dish.

Blend the butter with the tarragon and mustard and dot the fish with this mixture. Season and bake in a moderate oven (190 °C (375 °F), Reg. 5) for about 20 minutes. Pour over the cream and continue to bake for a further 10 minutes.

Serve with boiled potatoes and a robust vegetable such as ratatouille or sliced beetroot baked in a cheese sauce.

Baked Fillets of Whiting or Bass Dutch Style

The flavourings of fish and bacon are so companionable that it is a pity they are not joined together more often. In this recipe the fish fillets are curled up and cooked on a bed of very fat bacon and onion which gives a delicious flavour to otherwise fairly anonymous fish.

Serves 6

6 thin slices salt pork or very fat streaky bacon rashers,
   rind removed
1 onion
2 bay leaves
8 small fillets whiting, bass or other white fish
85 g (3 oz) butter
4 cream crackers
3 tablespoons flour

Salt and white pepper
285 ml ($\frac{1}{2}$ pint) milk
2 tablespoons finely chopped parsley

Finely chop the slices of salt pork or streaky bacon. Peel and very finely chop the onion. Arrange the onion and pork in the bottom of a well-greased baking dish. Add the bay leaves and cover with the fillets, neatly rolled and secured with toothpicks.

Melt 14 g ($\frac{1}{2}$ oz) butter, add the crackers (crushed with a rolling pin) and toss over a medium high heat until the crumbs are well buttered.

Soften the remaining butter and mix to a paste with 1 tablespoon flour. Season lightly and spread the mixture over the rolled up fillets. Sprinkle over the buttered crumbs and bake in a moderate oven (180 °C (350 °F), Reg. 4) for about 25 minutes or until the fish fillets are tender. Take the fillets out with tongs, remove the toothpicks and arrange the fillets on a heated serving dish. Surround with the bacon and onion.

Put $1\frac{1}{2}$ tablespoons fat from the juices in the baking dish into a small saucepan with 2 tablespoons flour. Mix well over a medium heat and then gradually add the milk, stirring continually until the sauce comes to the boil and is thick and smooth. Season, mix in the parsley and simmer for 3 minutes.

Pour the sauce over the fish fillets and serve at once.

Savoury Fish Creams

Serves 6 as a main course

225 g (8 oz) cooked white fish fillets, skin removed (any firm-fleshed white fish: John Dory, pollock, coley, whiting, etc.)
225 g (8 oz) prawns
142 ml ($\frac{1}{4}$ pint) white sauce (see page 212)
1 egg white

Salt and freshly ground black pepper
Pinch of cayenne and pinch of mace
142 ml ($\frac{1}{4}$ pint) cream
28 g (1 oz) melted butter
Cardinal sauce (see page 230)

Pound the fish, melted butter and two-thirds of the prawns until smooth (or purée in a liquidiser or food processor). Add the white sauce and egg white and mix until really smooth (this can also be done by machine). Season with salt, pepper and a pinch of cayenne and mace. Whip the cream until just stiff and fold it into the fish mixture. Divide the remaining prawns between six well-buttered cocotte or ramekin dishes and top with the fish mixture.

Cover the tops of the ramekins with circles of buttered greaseproof paper, place in a baking tin half filled with hot water and cook it in a moderate oven (180 °C (350 °F), Reg. 4) for 30 minutes.

Turn the moulds on to a hot dish and pour over a hot Cardinal sauce.

Whole Baked Fish with Fennel and Angel Sauce

1 red fish, about 1.8 kg (4 lb) in weight (or use 2 bass
   or grey mullet)
1 fennel root
6 spring onions
2 stalks celery
3 tablespoons oil
Salt and freshly ground black pepper

Clean and scale the fish and remove the gills. Trim and slice the fennel root. Cut the spring onions in half lengthwise. Thinly slice the celery. Blanch the vegetables in boiling salted water for 10 minutes and drain them well.

Place the fish on well-oiled foil, top with the vegetables, season and pour over the remaining oil. Fold the foil up neatly to make an airtight packet and bake the fish in a moderate oven (180 °C (350 °F), Reg. 4) for about 30 minutes for two smaller fish and about 45 minutes for a larger fish.

Transfer the fish to a serving dish and serve with the following sauce.

Angel sauce

This also goes well with plainly cooked poached or baked fish dishes.

> 25 mm (1 in) fresh ginger
> 2 cloves garlic
> 1 lemon
> 1 tablespoon olive oil
> 285 ml ($\frac{1}{2}$ pint) good fish stock (see page 67)
> 1 tablespoon tomato purée
> 1 teaspoon crushed green peppercorns
> 1 tablespoon cornflour

Peel and finely chop the ginger. Peel and finely chop or crush the garlic. Slice the lemon and remove the pips. Heat the oil, add the ginger and garlic and cook over a low heat until the garlic is soft and transparent. Add the stock, tomato purée, lemon and peppercorns, bring to the boil and simmer for 30 minutes or until the lemon is really soft. Blend the cornflour to a smooth paste with a little water. Add the cornflour mixture to the sauce and stir over a medium high heat until the sauce thickens and becomes transparent and shining. Check the seasoning before serving.

Crispolini

Serves 4

> 8 pancakes
> 340 g (12 oz) white fish fillets, skin and bones removed
>   (coley, bream, bass, etc.)
> 425 ml ($\frac{3}{4}$ pint) milk

28 g (1 oz) butter
28 g (1 oz) plain flour
Salt and freshly ground black pepper
85 g (3 oz) grated cheese
4 firm ripe tomatoes
1 tablespoon lemon juice

Put the fish into a shallow saucepan, cover with the milk and bring to the boil. Simmer for about 5 minutes or until the fish is just tender and will flake with a fork. Drain off and reserve the liquid; flake the fish.

Melt the butter in a small saucepan. Add the flour and mix well. Gradually add the liquid, stirring continually over a medium high heat until the sauce is thick and smooth. Season, add half the cheese and simmer for 3 minutes.

Scald the tomatoes, slide off skins, remove the seeds and cores and chop the flesh. Add to the sauce with the lemon juice, season and fold in the flaked fish.

Fill the pancakes with the fish mixture, roll up neatly and place in a lightly greased baking dish. Sprinkle over the remaining cheese and bake in a moderate oven (190 °C (375 °F), Reg. 5) for 20 minutes or until the cheese has melted and is golden brown and the dish is thoroughly hot.

Scalloped Queens

Serves 4

450 g (1 lb) queens
4 cream crackers
113 g (4 oz) butter
113 g (4 oz) fresh white breadcrumbs
Salt and freshly ground black pepper
$\frac{1}{2}$ teaspoon lemon juice
142 ml ($\frac{1}{4}$ pint) single cream

Remove any black veins from the queens. Crush the crackers coarsely with a rolling pin. Melt the butter, add the cracker crumbs and the breadcrumbs and mix well. Season the queens, add the lemon juice and mix lightly. Place a layer of crumbs in four small buttered baking dishes, cover with the queens and half the cream. Top with the remaining crumbs, pour over the remaining cream and bake in a moderately hot oven (200 °C (400 °F), Reg. 6) for about 15 minutes until the mixture is bubbling and the topping crisp and golden brown.

Fish with Vegetable Sauce

Serves 4–6

900 g (2 lb) red fish, bream, bass or grey mullet
1 carrot
1 stalk celery
1 medium onion
450 g (1 lb) ripe tomatoes
1 tablespoon olive or vegetable oil
Salt and freshly ground black pepper
1 bay leaf
Pinch dried thyme
4 tablespoons breadcrumbs
28 g (1 oz) butter

Fillet the fish and remove the skin; or ask your fishmonger to do this for you.

Peel and roughly chop the carrot. Slice the celery. Peel and thinly slice the onion. Scald the tomatoes, slide off skins and roughly chop the flesh.

Heat the oil in a saucepan. Add the onion, carrot and celery and cook over a low heat, stirring, until all the oil has been absorbed. Add the tomatoes, pour in just enough water to cover, season and add the herbs. Bring to the boil and simmer for about 15 minutes or until the vegetables are really soft. Remove the bay leaf and purée the vegetables.

Place the fish in a greased baking dish. Spread the sauce over, sprinkle on the breadcrumbs and dot with small pieces of butter. Bake the fish in a moderate oven (190 °C (375 °F), Reg. 5) for 30 minutes.

Cut each fillet in half and serve with new or mashed potatoes and a green vegetable.

Friday Pancakes

This was one of our New Year's inventions. I had four small roach and a grey mullet in the freezer and had decided to turn them into a fish soup to have as a first course. Just as I was about to start I remembered I also had eight pancakes in the freezer; there were eight of us dining that night so the fish soup suddenly became a starter of stuffed savoury pancakes that, because I had no Cheddar, Gruyère or Parmesan cheese, were topped with grated Derbyshire Sage instead. The combination was delicious and is now one of my stock light main courses or fairly substantial starters. For convenience I would recommend making this dish from filleted fish. Use any well-flavoured white-fleshed fish.

Serves 4 as a main course; 8 as a starter

8 small pancakes
450 g (1 lb) fish fillets, skin removed
Court bouillon or fish stock (see pages 66, 67)
85 g (3 oz) butter
Juice of 1 lemon
142 ml ($\frac{1}{4}$ pint) single cream
Salt and freshly ground black pepper (or for a special
    occasion use $\frac{1}{2}$ teaspoon crushed red or green
    peppercorns)
85 g (3 oz) grated Derbyshire Sage cheese

Lightly grease a baking dish, lay the fillets in it and cover with *court bouillon* or fish stock. Bake in a moderate oven (180 °C (350 °F), Reg. 4) for about 20 minutes or until the flesh is just tender and will flake when pierced with a fork. Drain the liquid and measure off 4 tablespoons. Flake the fish.

Melt the butter in a saucepan. Add the flaked fish, lemon juice and measured fish liquid and cook over a high heat for just a few minutes until the liquid has been absorbed. Lower the heat, stir in the cream, season and remove from the heat at once. Do not stir more than you have to – the fish should still be in flakes and not mushy.

Fill the pancakes with the fish and roll them up neatly. Arrange in a greased baking dish and sprinkle over the cheese. Put under the grill set on a medium heat and cook until the cheese has melted and the pancakes are hot through.

Gurnard Stuffed with Ham and Apples

Serves 4

4 gurnard
1 large cooking apple
2 teaspoons lemon juice
170 g (6 oz) ham
57 g (2 oz) fresh white or brown breadcrumbs
57 g (2 oz) softened butter
Salt and freshly ground black pepper
4 tablespoons olive oil
8 thin slices lemon

Clean and gut the gurnard and leave them whole.

Peel and grate the apple and sprinkle it with lemon juice to prevent it browning. Mince the ham through the fine blades of a mincing machine. Combine the apple with the ham and breadcrumbs and mix in the softened butter. Season the mixture and stuff the cavities of the gurnard with it.

Cut four pieces of foil large enough to wrap each fish in. Smear the foil with cooking oil, place the stuffed fish in the centre of the foil and pour over the olive oil. Season lightly, top each fish with 2 slices of lemon and wrap each fish loosely in the foil.

Bake the fish in a moderately hot oven (200 °C (400 °F), Reg. 6) for about 20–30 minutes depending on size, until they are tender and the flesh is beginning to flake away from the bones.

Serve with baked potatoes and a green vegetable, either in the foil cases or carefully transferred to a serving dish.

Red Fish, Leek and Mushroom Pie

Another of those good rich fish pies that make a really nutritious meal.

Serves 4–6

1 red fish (about 900 g (2 lb) in weight), or 450 g (1 lb)
  cooked white fish, skinned and off the bone
3 medium leeks
57 g (2 oz) very small button mushrooms
85 g (3 oz) butter
2 tablespoons flour
285 ml ($\frac{1}{2}$ pint) milk
85 g (3 oz) Cheddar cheese
2 tablespoons white wine
Salt and freshly ground black pepper
450 g (1 lb) potatoes

Ask your fishmonger to clean the fish and remove the head (this can be used to make fish stock). Oil a steamer or metal colander to go on top of a saucepan. Place the fish in it and cook over gently boiling water for about 20 minutes until it is just tender and the flesh will flake. Remove the fish from the pan and leave to cool.

Clean the leeks and cut into slices. Wipe the mushrooms with a damp cloth if necessary. Remove the skin and bones from the fish and flake the flesh.

Melt two-thirds of the butter, add the leeks and cook over a low heat until soft and transparent (stir every now and then to prevent sticking). Add the mushrooms and cook over a low heat, stirring, for 3 minutes. Shake over the flour, mix well and gradually blend in the milk, stirring continually over a medium high heat until the sauce comes to the boil and is thick and smooth. Add the cheese, mix well and stir until the cheese has melted. Blend in the wine, season and fold in the fish. Put the mixture into a pie dish.

Peel the potatoes and cut into thin slices. Arrange in overlapping layers on top of the fish and dot with the remaining butter. Sprinkle with a little salt and pepper and bake in a moderately hot oven (200 °C (400 °F), Reg. 6) for 10 minutes then lower the heat to moderate (180 °C (350 °F), Reg. 4) and continue to cook for a further 30 minutes until the potatoes are tender and golden brown on the top.

Serve with a green vegetable or with a salad.

Note: Only 57 g (2 oz) of cheese can be put in the sauce and the remainder sprinkled over the potatoes.

John Dory Véronique

Even though sole is so expensive these days there is no reason to forgo this delicious classical French sauce. John Dory fillets make an excellent substitute (or you could use fillets from fairly large dabs or megrim sole). The dish can be made from any white grapes but since large grapes will have to be skinned and have the pips removed I prefer to cook this dish when the tiny seedless grapes are in season.

Serves 4

8 fillets John Dory, skin removed
Salt and white pepper
8 spring onions
85 g (3 oz) butter
142 ml ($\frac{1}{4}$ pint) water
142 ml ($\frac{1}{4}$ pint) dry white wine
2 tablespoons flour
142 ml ($\frac{1}{4}$ pint) milk

1 egg yolk
4 tablespoons double cream
225 g ($\frac{1}{2}$ lb) seedless white grapes

Roll up the fillets of fish and secure them neatly with toothpicks. Sprinkle with a little salt and pepper. Trim the spring onions, remove the green stalks and thinly slice the white part. Generously grease a baking dish with some of the butter, sprinkle the onions over the bottom and place the fillets on top. Pour over the water and wine, cover with foil and bake in a fairly hot oven (220 °C (425 °F), Reg. 7) for 10 minutes until the fillets are barely cooked. Strain off the cooking liquid. Transfer the fillets to a heated serving dish, remove the toothpicks carefully so as not to break up the fish and keep them warm while making the sauce.

Melt 28 g (1 oz) butter in a small heavy saucepan. Add the flour and mix well. Gradually blend in the milk, stirring continually over a medium high heat until the sauce is thick and smooth. Beat in the cooking liquid, bring to the boil and simmer for 2 minutes.

Beat the egg yolk with 2 tablespoons of the cream until smooth. Beat remaining cream until thick. Add the egg yolk and cream mixture to the sauce and cook over a very low heat, stirring all the time until the sauce is thick and satiny. Add the remaining butter and stir until melted. Fold in the grapes and the whipped cream and pour the sauce over the fish fillets.

Place the dish under a hot grill just long enough to brown lightly.

Mackerel with Potatoes and Onions, Swedish Style

Serves 4

Salt and freshly ground black pepper
8 mackerel fillets
4 large potatoes

2 onions
57 g (2 oz) butter
142 ml ($\frac{1}{4}$ pint) cream

Season the mackerel fillets. Peel and thinly slice the potatoes. Peel and very thinly slice the onions. Arrange the mackerel fillets diagonally in a well-greased baking dish with the slices of potato and onions in between. Melt the butter, season it lightly and pour over the ingredients in the dish. Pour over the cream, cover tightly with foil and bake in a moderate oven (180 °C (350 °F), Reg. 4) for 1 hour or until the potatoes are tender.

Serve with a green vegetable.

Stuffed Whiting

Serves 2–3

1 900-g (2-lb) whiting
6 tablespoons parsley and thyme stuffing
142 ml ($\frac{1}{4}$ pint) water
57 g (2 oz) dried apricots
1 egg, beaten
57 g (2 oz) melted butter
Salt and pepper
142 ml ($\frac{1}{4}$ pint) double cream

Clean the whiting and remove the fins, head and tail. Cut pockets with a sharp pointed knife on either side of the backbone.

Mix the stuffing with the water. Finely chop or mince the apricots and mix them into the stuffing with the beaten egg and half the butter. Season and stuff into the pockets cut on either side of the backbone and into the stomach cavity. Season the fish and place stomach side down in a buttered dish. Melt the remaining butter and pour it over the fish. Cover lightly with a piece of buttered paper and bake in a moderately hot oven (200 °C (400 °F), Reg. 6) for 20 minutes.

Pour over the cream and put under a hot grill until the cream is bubbling and golden.

Serve at once with mashed or boiled potatoes and a green salad.

Cold fish dishes

Some of my favourite fish dishes are those served cold.
For one thing cold fish dishes tend to be a bit unusual and I
like the unusual, expecially when it brings out the flavour
and subtle texture of ingredients. The following pages include
fish dishes to serve as first courses, as part of a buffet or as
light and sophisticated lunch or supper dishes.

Fish Mousse with Prawns

This easily made and excellent mousse can be made with
any quality white fish. I have used coley, bass and bream
with excellent results. It makes a good centrepiece for a
cold buffet or a main dish for a summer party. As a first
course this would easily serve ten people; main course
servings are a little more difficult to pin down because it
depends, to a certain extent, what you are planning to serve
with the mousse.

675 g (1½ lb) cooked white fish fillets, skin and bones
removed
4 tablespoons mayonnaise
Salt and white pepper
2 teaspoons lemon juice
Few drops Tabasco
28 g (1 oz) gelatine
142 ml (¼ pint) water
2 egg whites
570 ml (1 pint) double cream
4 tablespoons sunflower or olive oil
1 tablespoon white wine vinegar
½ teaspoon Dijon mustard
Freshly ground black pepper
1 tablespoon finely chopped parsley
1 tablespoon finely chopped chives
A little finely chopped dill or fresh tarragon
170 g (6 oz) peeled prawns

Mince the fish through the fine blades of a mincing machine.
Mix the fish with the mayonnaise, season with salt and

white pepper and mix in the lemon juice and a little Tabasco sauce. Soften the gelatine in the water and mix over a very low heat until dissolved. Add the gelatine mixture to the fish and mix well.

Beat the egg whites until stiff. Beat the cream until thick. Fold the cream and then the egg whites into the fish base and mix lightly. Turn the mixture into an oiled ring mould and chill in the refrigerator until set firm.

Combine the oil, vinegar and mustard, season with salt and freshly ground black pepper and mix well. Add the parsley, chives and tarragon or dill and mix in the prawns. Chill the mixture in the refrigerator.

Turn the mousse out of the mould and fill the centre with the dressed prawns.

Variations

Fill the centre with one of the fish cocktails on pages 190–191. Or economise and fill it with some watercress dipped into a vinaigrette dressing.

Brunswick Salad

Serves 6 as a first course

2 smoked mackerel
450 g (1 lb) waxy potatoes
1 cooking apple
5 tablespoons sunflower oil
2 tablespoons lemon juice
1 tablespoon finely chopped chives
Salt and freshly ground black pepper
Pinch turmeric
1 small green pepper

Remove the skin and bones of the mackerel and roughly flake the flesh. Boil the potatoes in their skins until just tender and drain well. Leave to cool, remove the skins and

cut the flesh into small dice. Peel and dice the apple, removing the core.

Combine the oil, lemon juice and chives, mix well and
season. Mix in a little turmeric to give a pleasant yellow hue
to the dressing. Remove the core and seeds of the green
pepper and finely chop the flesh.

Combine the fish, potatoes, apple and green pepper, pour
over the dressing and toss lightly. Pile the salad on lettuce
leaves (or serve in scooped out lemon cups) and serve well
chilled with hot toast and butter.

Lemon Cases Stuffed with Smoked Mackerel

Serves 6

6 large thin-skinned lemons
225 g ($\frac{1}{2}$ lb) smoked mackerel fillets
1 teaspoon Dijon mustard
113 g (4 oz) butter
Salt, freshly ground black pepper and a pinch
    cayenne
12 bay leaves, preferably fresh

Cut a slice from the top of each lemon and a sliver from the
bottom so that they will stand up. Use a grapefruit spoon to
hollow out the flesh from the inside of the lemons. Remove
the skin from the mackerel and pound the fillets to a smooth
paste with the mustard and butter. Season the pâté with
salt, pepper and a pinch of cayenne and fill the lemon cases
with it. Return the top of the lemons, making a small slit
in the top of each, and stick 2 bay leaves into it to look like
lemon leaves. Chill the lemon cases well before serving with
thin slices of buttered brown bread.

Marinated Devilled Sprats

I discovered this way of serving sprats purely by chance. I
had cooked sprats for a dinner party that, at the very last

minute, did not materialise. Rather than throw them away I covered them with a marinade of a French dressing flavoured with lemon juice as well as a little white wine vinegar and left them to steep overnight. The dish, eaten cold the next day, was extremely good. It should be made with small sprats rather than those about 125–150 mm (5–6 in) long, and do ensure that the fish are really well cooked. They should be so crisp that the bones melt in your mouth.

Serves 4 as a starter

450 g (1 lb) sprats
Flour, salt, pepper and cayenne
142 ml ($\frac{1}{4}$ pint) sunflower oil
2 tablespoons white wine or cider vinegar
Juice of $\frac{1}{2}$ lemon
1 teaspoon made English mustard or Dijon mustard
1 tablespoon finely chopped chives
1 tablespoon finely chopped parsley

Remove the heads and tails of the sprats. Season the flour with salt, pepper and cayenne and coat the fish in it. Heat the oil until a haze rises from it, add the sprats (do not attempt to cook too many at one time) and cook until really crisp and golden. Drain the sprats on kitchen paper to remove all excess oil.

Combine the oil, vinegar, lemon juice and mustard in a screw-topped jar. Add the chives and parsley, season and shake to mix well.

Arrange the sprats in a shallow dish (they should still be warm) pour over the dressing and chill in a refrigerator for at least 8 hours but preferably overnight. Serve well chilled with brown bread and butter.

Whiting or other White Fish alla Bagna Cauda

This is a marvellous summer dish. You can serve it hot, or leave to cool and then serve well chilled so that the flavours of the ingredients have time to infuse the fish. Accompany with a green salad and crusty bread.

Serves 4

1.1 kg (2½ lb) whiting
3 cloves garlic
1 large onion
8 anchovy fillets
1 red pepper
3 tablespoons sunflower oil
142 ml (¼ pint) double cream
Freshly ground black pepper

Steam the whiting until just tender. Remove the skin and bones and flake the fish into large pieces while it is still warm.

Peel and crush the garlic. Peel the onion, cut it into thin slices and separate into rings. Pound the anchovies to a paste. Put the pepper under a hot grill and cook, turning it every now and then, until the skin blackens and can be removed. Remove the skin, halve and remove the core and seeds and cut the flesh into thin strips.

Heat the oil. Add the garlic and onion and cook over a low heat until soft and transparent. Add the pepper and the anchovy paste and continue to cook over a low heat for 10 minutes. Stir in the cream and season with pepper – do not allow to boil.

Arrange the whiting in a serving dish and pour over the sauce.

Baked Sprats

This makes one of the best and cheapest ways I know of to start off a summer meal. The sprats are cooked like soused herrings or mackerel and their bones should melt in the mouth.

Serves 4

900 g (2 lb) sprats
Salt and freshly ground black pepper
Pinch mace and nutmeg
1 onion
4 bay leaves
285 ml ($\frac{1}{2}$ pint) white wine vinegar
28 g (1 oz) butter
Lettuce leaves
Parsley sprigs

Remove the heads and tails of the sprats. Wash the sprats under cold water and pat dry on kitchen paper. Arrange head to tail in a shallow baking dish, season them well and sprinkle with nutmeg and ground mace.

Peel and thinly slice the onion and divide it into rings. Place on top of the sprats and top with the bay leaves. Pour over the vinegar and enough water to cover, and dot with butter.

Cover tightly with buttered foil and bake in a moderate oven (180 °C (350 °F), Reg. 4) for 1 hour or until the sprats and their bones are soft. Leave them to cool and then chill thoroughly in a refrigerator.

Drain off the liquid and serve the sprats on a bed of lettuce leaves (I pile mine in a pyramid), garnish with sprigs of fresh parsley and serve with sauces like Ravigote or Tomato (pages 213 and 222).

Cold Marinated Red Mullet

There are many classic recipes for this way of cooking red mullet and I have never been able to make up my mind which is the best. This is a slight variation on the one in Elizabeth David's great cookery book *Italian Food*. It makes a very sophisticated dish to start a summer dinner party, but the mullet must be fairly small and very fresh.

Serves 4

4 red mullet
Flour
Salt and freshly ground black pepper
Olive or sunflower oil
1 onion
2 cloves garlic
142 ml ($\frac{1}{4}$ pint) dry white wine
1 tablespoon white wine vinegar
4 tablespoons water
12 leaves mint
1 small lemon

Clean the mullet, leaving the livers in place but removing the gills. Season some flour and roll the mullet in it until well coated. Heat about 6 mm ($\frac{1}{4}$ in) oil in a frying pan, add the mullet and cook over a low heat for about 5 minutes on each side until they are just cooked through. Remove to a shallow serving dish.

Peel and thinly slice the onion. Peel and crush the garlic. Add the onion and garlic to the juices in the pan and cook over a low heat until the onion is soft and transparent. Add the white wine, vinegar and water, bring to the boil and cook over a high heat until the sauce has reduced by about a third. Leave to cool.

Very finely chop the mint and spread it over the fish. Cut the lemon into thin slices and remove the pips. Spread the lemon slices on top of the mullet and pour over the sauce.

Chill the dish in the refrigerator for at least 2 hours before serving with brown bread and butter.

Smoked Mackerel and Cream Cheese Pâté

I used to pooh pooh this pâté when my friends told me how marvellous it was. I thought it must be too rich and rather sickly. Then I had it one night at a dinner party and I had to admit that I was quite wrong – the taste of the cream cheese counteracts the somewhat rich texture and flavour of the mackerel. It makes a first-rate starter.

Serves 4

1 medium smoked mackerel on the bone
Juice ½ lemon
113 g (4 oz) cream cheese
Salt and a pinch of paprika
Freshly ground black pepper or 1½ teaspoons crushed
   green peppercorns

Remove the skin and bones from the mackerel and pound the flesh to a smooth paste with the lemon juice in a mortar, or purée it in a blender or food processor. Add the cheese to the paste and beat with a wooden spoon until the ingredients are all well blended. Season with salt and paprika and pack into a small pot. Top the pâté with coarsely grated black pepper or crushed green peppercorns and serve well chilled with hot toast or hot French bread.

Marinated Fish

This is a delicious West Indian recipe which I first tasted in Montego Bay, Jamaica, where they have some of the best fish in the world.

Serves 4

675 g (1½ lb) John Dory fillets, skin removed
1 onion

2 cloves garlic
3 pieces of stem ginger
142 ml ($\frac{1}{4}$ pint) fresh lime or lemon juice
2 tablespoons ginger wine
142 ml ($\frac{1}{4}$ pint) dry white wine
$\frac{1}{4}$ teaspoon chilli powder
Salt and freshly ground black pepper
Cayenne pepper

Cut the fish into 25-mm (1-in) pieces. Peel and very thinly slice the onion and divide into rings. Peel and crush the garlic. Cut the ginger into very, very thin slices. Place the fish in a shallow dish and top with ginger, onion and garlic.

Combine the lime or lemon juice, ginger wine, white wine, chilli powder, salt and pepper, and mix well. Pour the marinade over the fish and refrigerate for at least 5 hours (preferably overnight) until the flesh of the fish turns opaque. Drain off most of the marinade, arrange the pieces of fish on some lettuce leaves and sprinkle with cayenne pepper. Serve well chilled with buttered brown bread.

Spiced Fish

Serves 4

2 grey mullet, filleted
1 onion
1 clove garlic
2 tablespoons olive or sunflower oil
$\frac{1}{2}$ teaspoon ground ginger
1 397-g (14-oz) tin tomatoes
1 tablespoon tomato purée
142 ml ($\frac{1}{4}$ pint) *court bouillon* (see page 66)
2 teaspoons lemon juice
1 teaspoon Worcestershire sauce
Salt and freshly ground black pepper
Black olives

Fillet the mullet and arrange in an oiled baking dish.

Peel and finely chop the onion. Peel and crush the garlic. Heat the oil in a saucepan, add the onion and garlic and cook over a low heat until the onion is soft and transparent. Mix in the ginger and continue to cook for a further minute. Add the tomatoes, tomato purée, *court bouillon*, lemon juice and Worcestershire sauce, mix well, bring to the boil and season. Simmer for 20 minutes.

Pour the sauce over the fish and bake the fillets in a moderate oven (180 °C (350 °F), Reg. 4) for about 20 minutes or until just cooked through. Remove from the oven and leave to cool.

Chill the dish thoroughly before serving with thin slices of buttered brown bread or hot French bread. Garnish with slices of large black olives.

Cocktail of Huss and Tomatoes

Serves 6

340 g (12 oz) huss
Court bouillon (see page 66)
142 ml ($\frac{1}{4}$ pint) mayonnaise
2 tablespoons tomato purée
2 teaspoons lemon juice
142 ml ($\frac{1}{4}$ pint) double cream
1 teaspoon made horseradish sauce
Worcestershire sauce and Tabasco sauce
Salt and freshly ground black pepper
2 hard-boiled eggs
2 large firm tomatoes
1 large or two small lettuce hearts
1 lemon
Paprika

Place the huss in a shallow pan, cover it with cold *court bouillon*, bring gently to the boil and lower the heat as soon as the liquid bubbles. Cover and cook very gently for about

10 minutes or until the fish is just cooked. Remove the fish, leave to cool and then flake into pieces.

Flavour the mayonnaise with the tomato purée and lemon juice and mix in the cream and horseradish. Add a little Worcestershire and Tabasco sauce and season if necessary. Chop the hard-boiled eggs. Peel the tomatoes, remove core and seeds and chop the flesh. Shred the lettuce hearts.

Divide the lettuce between four glass goblets. Fold the fish, tomatoes and hard-boiled eggs into the mayonnaise and spoon the mixture on top of the lettuce. Chill in a refrigerator for at least 30 minutes and serve with thin slices of buttered brown bread and a garnish of thin slices of lemon and a sprinkling of paprika.

Piquant Fish Cocktail

Don't tell your friends this is made from skate wings – the texture of the cooked skate is so similar to the white flesh of crab that it makes the perfect ingredient for a rather spicy fish cocktail to serve as a first course.

Serves 4

1 large skate wing
Court bouillon (see page 66)
1 teaspoon finely chopped parsley
1 teaspoon very finely chopped chives
$\frac{1}{2}$ teaspoon very finely chopped shallot
10 drops Tabasco sauce
1 teaspoon Worcestershire sauce
$\frac{1}{2}$ teaspoon dry mustard
2 tablespoons white wine vinegar
8 tablespoons tomato ketchup
$\frac{1}{2}$ teaspoon freshly grated horseradish root
4 tablespoons double cream
Shredded lettuce and sliced lemon to finish

Place the skate wing in a saucepan, cover with cold *court bouillon*, bring slowly to the boil, cover and simmer slowly for 8 minutes. Remove the pan from the heat and leave to cool. Drain the fish, remove the skin and shred the flesh from the bones. Combine all the other ingredients and mix well. Add the shredded skate and toss lightly so that it is well coated with the sauce.

Place some shredded lettuce in the bottom of four glass goblets, top with the skate mixture and chill well before serving with a garnish of thin slices of lemon and some thin slices of buttered brown bread.

Smoked Fish and Tomato Rice Salad

This is a good summer salad, and not too expensive to serve as part of a buffet spread for an outdoor party. The quality and price of the smoked fish you use depends on your purse strings.

Serves 4

225 g (8 oz) smoked fish (smoked salmon, saithe, haddock, cod, mackerel, bloaters, etc.)
225 g (8 oz) long-grain rice
1 large packet (340 g (12 oz)) frozen mixed vegetables
6 firm ripe tomatoes
4 tablespoons olive or sunflower oil
2 tablespoons white wine vinegar
1 teaspoon made English mustard
Salt and freshly ground black pepper
Pinch sugar
1 tablespoon finely chopped parsley
1 tablespoon finely chopped chives
Bunch watercress

Cook the smoked fish if necessary (fish like smoked haddock, cod, etc. will have to be steamed, but smoked salmon, saithe and mackerel, etc. are ready to serve). Flake or finely chop the fish. Cook the rice in boiling salted water until just tender and drain well. Cook the vegetables in boiling salted water until just tender and drain. Scald the tomatoes, slide off the skins, remove the core and seeds and chop the flesh, reserving any juice.

Combine the oil, vinegar, mustard, seasoning and sugar and mix well. Add the tomatoes and tomato juice and mix in the rice, vegetables, fish, parsley and chives, tossing the mixture lightly. Check the seasoning, chill and serve in a ring of watercress leaves.

White Fish and Rice Salad

This is a never-ending summer favourite of mine. No one ever seems to get tired of it; perhaps because it never tastes the same twice. Don't just stick to this recipe; use whatever you have in the refrigerator.

Serves 4

450 g (1 lb) white fish fillet, skin removed (coley, etc.,
    or use a fish like John Dory or grey mullet)
225 g (8 oz) long-grain rice
1 clove garlic
4 tablespoons olive or sunflower oil
1½ tablespoons white wine vinegar
½ teaspoon Dijon mustard
Salt and freshly ground black pepper
1 green pepper
1 red pepper
2 large ripe tomatoes
3 spring onions

Steam the fish to the point where it will just flake with a fork. Leave to cool and then flake.

Cook the rice in boiling salted water until just tender and drain well. Leave until cool but not cold. Peel and crush the garlic and mix it with the oil, vinegar, mustard and seasoning. Remove the core and seeds of the green and red peppers and finely chop the flesh. Scald the tomatoes, slide off the skins, remove the core and seeds and chop the flesh. Finely chop the spring onions.

Combine the rice, fish, peppers, tomatoes and onions, and pour over the dressing. Toss lightly so as not to break up the fish more than is absolutely necessary and chill the salad before serving.

Huss with Vinaigrette and Capers

I had a dish similar to this at the famous Horn of Plenty Restaurant in Gunnislake, near Tavistock one evening. It was sharp and a good dish to get even the most jaded of appetites going for more excitements to follow.

Serves 4

795 g ($1\frac{3}{4}$ lb) huss
Flour
Salt and freshly ground black pepper
Pinch paprika
Olive or sunflower oil for frying
4 tablespoons olive oil
1 tablespoon white wine vinegar
1 teaspoon Dijon mustard
Pinch dried basil or 1 teaspoon finely chopped fresh
    basil
1 tablespoon finely chopped capers
1 tinned pimento

Cut the huss into 50-mm (2-in) pieces. Season some flour with salt, pepper and a little paprika and roll the pieces of fish in it. Heat 13 mm ($\frac{1}{2}$ in) oil in a frying pan, add the fish and cook over a moderately high heat until the fish is golden brown and cooked through. Drain on kitchen paper and leave to cool, then arrange in a shallow serving dish.

Combine the oil, vinegar, French mustard and basil in a screw-topped jar and shake to mix well. Season, mix in the capers and pour the sauce over the fish. Garnish with strips of red pimento and chill for at least 2 hours before serving.

Whiting Fillets à l'Indienne

I consider this a most sophisticated and elegant dish. Serve it cold for a rather substantial first course, or a perfect summer main course. When I first had the dish it was made with sole, but whiting, usually very good value, makes a very acceptable substitute.

Serves 8 as a first course

4 small whiting
225 g (8 oz) long-grain rice
Salt and freshly ground black pepper
1 green pepper
113 g (4 oz) frozen peas
2 tomatoes
3 tablespoons olive oil
1½ teaspoons white wine vinegar
28 g (1 oz) butter
Milk
1 small onion
2 teaspoons curry powder
1 teaspoon tomato purée
5 tablespoons red wine
142 ml (¼ pint) water
1 bay leaf
Pinch of sugar
½ teaspoon lemon juice
425 ml (¾ pint) mayonnaise
1 tablespoon apricot jam
3 tablespoons double cream
1 tinned pimento

Fillet and skin the whiting – or ask your fishmonger to do it. (Use the bones and trimmings to make a fish stock or *court bouillon* for another dish.)

Put the rice into a saucepan and pour over enough cold water to come about 19 mm (¾ in) above it. Add a little salt, bring to the boil, stir well, cover tightly and simmer for about 20 minutes, by which time the water should all have been absorbed by the rice, which should be tender.

Remove the core and seeds of the pepper and finely chop the flesh. Cook the peas in boiling salted water until just tender and drain well. Scald the tomatoes, slide off skins, remove the cores and seeds and chop the flesh. Add the peas, pepper and tomatoes to the rice, pour over 2 table-spoons of olive oil and the vinegar, season, mix well and leave to cool.

Place the fish fillets in a shallow pan. Dot with the butter, season and pour over enough milk to cover. Bring slowly to the boil and simmer gently for about 5 minutes or until the fillets are just tender. Drain and leave to cool.

Peel and finely chop the onion. Heat the remaining olive oil, add the onion and cook over a low heat until soft and transparent. Add the curry powder and mix well. Add the tomato purée, wine, water and bay leaf, bring to the boil, add a pinch of sugar and the lemon juice and season. Simmer for 10 minutes and purée through a fine sieve. Leave to cool. Add the curry mixture, a little at a time, to the mayonnaise and mix in the apricot jam and the cream, whipped until just stiff.

Arrange the rice in a shallow dish, place the fillets on top and mask them with the curry mayonnaise. Garnish with thin strips of tinned pimento.

Squid Salad

You may find the quantities I give for this dish are on the generous side; that is because I love this salad so much. I like to serve it as a starter, but you can also combine the squid with other cooked and flaked fish to make an ex-tremely good-sized seafood salad. Try using the same amount of squid, 340 g ($\frac{3}{4}$ lb) cooked and flaked white fish and 170 g (6 oz) peeled prawns.

Serves 4

675 g (1½ lb) squid
9 tablespoons olive or sunflower oil
Juice of 1 lemon
Salt and freshly ground black pepper
3 spring onions
3 firm ripe tomatoes
1 green pepper
1½ tablespoons white wine vinegar
Pinch of cayenne

Clean the squid (see page 37), cutting the bodies into thin rings. Pour over 2 tablespoons oil and the lemon juice, season and leave to stand for 1 hour. Drain well and pat dry.

Clean and thinly slice the onions. Scald the tomatoes, slide off skins, remove the core and seeds and chop the flesh. Remove the core and seeds of the green pepper and chop the flesh.

Heat a frying pan, add 3 tablespoons oil and when smoking throw in the squid. Cook over a high heat, stirring, for about 3 minutes or until tender. Drain on kitchen paper and leave to cool. Make a dressing from the remaining oil and white wine vinegar, seasoned with salt, pepper and cayenne. Add the squid, tomatoes, onions and green pepper and serve well chilled.

Lexington Cocktail

Serves 4

170 g (6 oz) huss off the bones
3 teaspoons lemon juice
142 ml (¼ pint) mayonnaise
2 tablespoons tomato ketchup
Few drops Tabasco and Worcestershire sauce
4 tablespoons double cream
Salt and freshly ground black pepper

1 avocado
2 tomatoes
2 tablespoons olive oil

Steam the huss for 10 minutes until tender, leave to cool and then cut into thin strips about 50 mm (2 in) long and 13 mm ($\frac{1}{2}$ in) wide.

Add 1 teaspoon of the lemon juice to the mayonnaise with the tomato ketchup and a few drops of Tabasco and Worcestershire sauce; mix well. Blend in the cream and season, if necessary.

Peel the avocado, remove the stone and cut the flesh into fine dice. Toss the avocado immediately in 1 teaspoon lemon juice to prevent it going brown. Scald the tomatoes, slide off skins, remove the core and seeds and chop the flesh.

Season the olive oil, add the avocado and remaining lemon juice, tomatoes and huss and toss lightly to mix. Spoon the huss and tomato/avocado mixture into the bottom of four glass goblets, spoon over the mayonnaise and chill before serving. If liked, garnish with very thin slices of lemon and serve with thin slices of buttered brown bread.

St Valentine's Smoked Mackerel

If you want to find the way to a man's heart try this very special starter next St Valentine's day. I can't guarantee that wedding bells will swing, but you'll certainly go up in his estimation after he has eaten this combination of smoked mackerel, apple purée and mayonnaise flavoured with horseradish.

Serves 4

4 smoked mackerel
Lettuce leaves
450 g (1 lb) potatoes
3 spring onions
142 ml ($\frac{1}{4}$ pint) cooked apple purée

1 tablespoon made horseradish sauce
285 ml ($\frac{1}{2}$ pint) mayonnaise
Salt and freshly ground black pepper
A little cayenne pepper

Remove the skin from the mackerel and neatly lift out the bones. Arrange the fillets on four plates on lettuce leaves. Cook the potatoes in their skins until just tender. Drain, cool and peel, then cut into small dice. Very finely chop the spring onions, separating the white and green part. Add the apple purée and horseradish sauce to the mayonnaise and mix well. Season and mix in the diced potatoes and the white part of the spring onions.

Spread the mayonnaise mixture over the mackerel fillets and sprinkle over the spring onion tops and a little cayenne. Serve well chilled with buttered brown bread.

Soused Fillets of Fish with Mayonnaise

Although one is more used to oily fish like herring or mackerel being soused, the process also succeeds with white fish, especially those that do not have a very strong flavour of their own. I have made this dish with fillets of pollock, red fish and imported carp with great success. Serve as a first course with thin slices of buttered brown bread.

Serves 4

4 fillets white fish (about 142 g (5 oz) each)
4 slices lemon
142 ml ($\frac{1}{4}$ pint) white wine
Bouquet garni
Salt and freshly ground black pepper
1 shallot
1 carrot
1 stick celery
1 pickled gherkin
2 teaspoons capers

4 tablespoons double cream
142 ml ($\frac{1}{4}$ pint) mayonnaise
Lettuce leaves
Paprika

Fold each fillet in half with a thin slice of lemon inside. Put the fish into a buttered baking dish, pour over the wine and enough cold water just to cover, add the bouquet garni and season. Cover the dish with buttered greaseproof paper or foil and bake in a moderate oven (180 °C (350 °F), Reg. 4) for about 20 minutes or until the fish is just tender (it is very important not to overcook).

Strain off the cooking liquid and remove the bouquet garni. Peel and very thinly slice the shallot and divide into rings. Peel and very thinly slice the carrot. Very thinly slice the celery. Very finely chop the gherkin and capers.

Add the shallot, carrot and celery to the cooking liquid, bring to the boil and boil until they are cooked. Strain the liquid over the fish and leave to cool. Reserve the vegetables and leave the fish to chill in a refrigerator for at least 2 hours before serving.

Beat the cream until stiff. Fold the cream into the mayonnaise with the vegetables, capers and gherkin, and season if necessary.

Strain off the liquid from the fish and arrange the fish on lettuce leaves. Top with the mayonnaise mixture and sprinkle with a little paprika pepper. Serve well chilled.

Monk Fish or Huss Niçoise

Serves 6 as a first course or 4 as a main course

340 g ($\frac{3}{4}$ lb) monk fish or huss
Court bouillon (see page 66)
1 small tin tuna fish
2 cos lettuces
3 tomatoes
8 spring onions

4 anchovy fillets
½ cucumber
170 g (6 oz) thin French beans
2 hard-boiled eggs
12 black olives
142 ml (¼ pint) French dressing

Place the fish in a shallow pan, cover with cold *court bouillon*, bring slowly to the boil and simmer gently until just cooked (about 10 minutes). Remove the fish and leave to cool. Flake the fish. Drain and flake the tuna.

Remove the outside leaves of the lettuces and cut the hearts into quarters. Peel the tomatoes and cut into quarters, remove the seeds. Cut the anchovy fillets in half lengthwise. Remove the peel from the cucumber and cut into 50-mm (2-in) lengths. Cut each chunk of cucumber into four lengthwise. Top and tail the beans. Quarter the hard-boiled eggs. Cook the French beans in boiling salted water until just tender, plunge into cold water and drain well.

Arrange the lettuces, cucumber, tomatoes, beans and spring onions on a serving dish and top with the hard-boiled eggs, anchovies, fish, tuna and olives. Pour over the French dressing, well seasoned, and serve well chilled with hot French bread.

Mackerel Shashimi

Serves 4

450 g (1 lb) very fresh mackerel fillets
142 ml (¼ pint) soy sauce
1½ tablespoons finely grated horseradish
Watercress and radishes

Remove the skin from the mackerel fillets and cut the fillets into very thin slices about 6 mm (¼ in) thick, cut on the diagonal. Arrange the slices in a fan on a serving dish and place a bowl of mixed soy sauce and horseradish in the centre. Garnish with watercress and radish. To eat the shashimi, pieces of fish should be picked up with chop-sticks or forks and dipped into the soy and horseradish sauce.

Marinated Mackerel with Avocados

Serves 4

2 small very fresh mackerel, filleted
4 tablespoons olive or good vegetable oil
Juice of 2 lemons
1 large ripe tomato
1 medium onion
1 small red chilli
Salt and freshly ground black pepper
1 large or 2 small avocados
6 stuffed olives
2 tablespoons finely chopped fresh coriander or celery leaves

Remove the skin of the mackerel fillets and cut the fillets into small cubes. Pour over the oil and lemon juice (reserving 1 tablespoon) and leave the fish to marinate for 2 hours.

Scald the tomato, drain and slide off the skin. Halve it, remove the core and seeds and finely chop the flesh. Peel and very finely chop the onion. Remove the core and seeds from the chilli and very finely chop the flesh.

Drain off the excess liquid from the mackerel, combine it with the tomato, onion and chilli, season and toss lightly.

Peel and halve the avocado and cut the flesh into thin slices. Dip the slices in the reserved lemon juice to prevent them browning and arrange in a circle, overlapping, around a serving dish. Pile the mackerel mixture in the centre, garnish with slices of stuffed olives and coriander leaves and serve well chilled with hot French bread and butter.

Swiss Salad

Swiss food has never been one of my favourites, but I am very fond of this simple salad. It is made with fish from the lakes when at home, but is equally good with white-fleshed sea fish such as brill, pollock, bass, grey mullet, or any other firm-fleshed white fish. But don't use coley – it flakes in too large portions.

Serves 4–6

450 g (1 lb) fish fillets, skin and bones removed
2 hard-boiled eggs
2 gherkins
4 anchovy fillets
1 teaspoon capers
2 teaspoons lemon juice
2 tablespoons olive oil
Freshly ground black pepper
1 tablespoon finely chopped chives
142 ml ($\frac{1}{4}$ pint) mayonnaise

Steam the fish (see page 60) until just tender. Leave to cool and then flake. Chop the hard-boiled eggs. Very finely chop the gherkins, anchovy fillets and capers.

Combine the lemon juice and oil, season with pepper, mix in the chives and then add the fish, eggs, gherkins, anchovy fillets and capers, and toss lightly. Press the mixture lightly into a small shallow serving dish, cover with mayonnaise and chill well before serving.

Note: For very special occasions I serve this salad in small ramekin dishes with the mayonnaise as a topping and a garnish of thin strips of tinned pimento wrapped rose-petal fashion around a stuffed olive.

Soused Mackerel and Marinated Mackerel

Soused or marinated mackerel make delicious cold dishes and the fish can also be drained and served in countless different ways as a first course or salad dish.

Do allow the fish to stand long enough for it to become thoroughly impregnated with the flavours of the marinade – leaving it for just one day or night is not enough for most dishes. Keep the fish in the refrigerator, covered, until required. Marinated mackerel, soaked in white wine, has a more delicate taste than soused mackerel, soaked in vinegar, and can be left for as long as a week for the full flavour to develop.

Soused Mackerel

Serves 6

6 medium mackerel
142 ml ($\frac{1}{4}$ pint) cider vinegar
1 tablespoon pickling spice
1 red chilli
3 bay leaves
1 large onion
Salt and freshly ground black pepper

Clean the fish, remove the head and tail and then remove the backbone, leaving the fish in one piece. Roll up the fish tightly, skin-side outwards, and pack them neatly in an oiled, fireproof baking dish. Combine the vinegar with the pickling spices, chilli and bay leaves. Peel and slice the onion and divide into rings. Arrange the onion on top of the mackerel, pour over the vinegar mixture, season, cover with foil and bake in a cool oven (150 °C (300 °F), Reg. 2) for $1\frac{1}{2}$ hours or until very tender. Cool and refrigerate for at least 48 hours before serving, well drained.

Marinated Mackerel

Serves 6

6 medium mackerel
1 teaspoon pickling spice

For the marinade
3 carrots
2 sticks celery
2 large onions
1 litre (1¾ pints) cheap dry white wine
1 clove garlic
1 teaspoon salt
1½ teaspoons black peppercorns
1 chilli
1 sprig dill (optional)
Fresh bay leaves or parsley sprigs

Peel and roughly chop the carrots. Clean and thickly slice the celery. Peel and slice the onions and divide into rings. Combine all the ingredients for the marinade, bring to the boil and cook over a high heat until reduced by half.

Clean the mackerel, removing their heads and tails, and take out the back bone leaving the fish in one piece. Place the fish in a shallow pan. Pour over the marinade, add the pickling spice and bring slowly to the boil. Remove from the heat and leave the fish to cool in the liquid.

Remove the skin from the fish and place the fillets in a clean dish. Pour over the strained marinade, cover with foil and leave to marinate in the refrigerator until required.

Strain off most of the liquid before serving and garnish the fish with fresh bay leaves or sprigs of parsley.

Sauces hot and cold

Almost any plainly cooked fish benefits from being served with a sauce, and the choice is wide: sharp sauces to contrast with rich, oily fish; subtle ones to complement delicately flavoured fish; strong-tasting ones to accompany the blander varieties; rich, luxury sauces to lift a humble fish into the realms of 'haute cuisine'.

Part of the object of this book is to revolutionise the serving of fish in British households, and this chapter will play a large part in reaching that goal since, when cooking fish, it is often the sauce that makes the finished dish memorable.

In order to keep its flavour and delicate texture, plain cooking – poaching, grilling, frying, steaming or baking – is often best for fish. In my opinion, such fish should always be accompanied by a sauce, chosen not to blanket the taste of the fish itself, but to complement it. Making a good sauce is not nearly so difficult as is commonly supposed, provided you follow the basic rules. And sauce-making can be the most creative form of cookery. The recipes given in this book, including many old favourites and some inventions of my own, can be used by you as ideas to develop with the addition of your own ingredients.

Most sauces are quick to prepare, and as the cooking of the actual fish is so simple, the combined operation should take no longer than producing a meat dish. Choosing which sauce to go with which fish, cooked by what method, is partly a matter of taste, but is based on balancing flavours, colour and texture.

GUIDELINES TO GOOD SAUCE-MAKING

1. A basic sauce must be absolutely smooth, so stir and beat it well to ensure it is completely free from lumps and as smooth as satin before you add any flavouring ingredients.

2. The finished sauce must have the right consistency: thick and creamy, but thin enough to pour. If it turns out too thick, add a little extra milk, stock, single cream, wine or cider. If too thin, mix a little butter to a smooth paste with

an equal amount of flour. Add this mixture (*beurre manié*) to the sauce in little pats and cook over a high heat, stirring continually, until thickened. Or beat an egg yolk into a little of the sauce, return the mixture to the pan and heat through, without boiling, stirring constantly.

3. Sauces thickened with eggs or cream must never be boiled once these have been added or they are liable to separate. Sauces thickened with flour must always be cooked long enough for the floury taste to disappear; at least 5 minutes.

4. Always add seasonings, concentrated flavourings and herbs with a light hand – you can always add more but you can't take away. Use white pepper for white or light-coloured sauces and for mayonnaise to avoid a speckly look, but otherwise black pepper is preferable as it has more flavour.

5. Pay special attention to the colour of a sauce; as fish is usually white, fish sauces should be on the colourful side. A green sauce should be really green, not greyish, and if the herb used hasn't provided enough colour a couple of drops of green vegetable colouring are permissible; but no more. Again, a pink sauce made with rosé wine or prawns can be strengthened with a tiny drop of red colouring. To improve the colour of a rich red or brown sauce add a little tomato purée, mushroom ketchup, soy sauce or reduced brown stock. A basically white sauce should have a 'glow' derived from cream, egg yolks or cheese, and can often be improved by a garnish: sieved hard-boiled egg yolks, strips of tinned pimento or halved black olives.

6. Whenever possible use fresh herbs; the flavour is infinitely better. If there is no alternative to dried, soak them in a little warm lemon juice to bring out the flavour.

7. Always make a sauce at the last possible moment before serving; the fresher the sauce the better it will taste. If it must wait for a while, cover the surface with greaseproof paper or cling film to prevent a skin forming.

UTENSILS FOR SAUCE-MAKING

The basic essential for making good sauces is a small, really good-quality saucepan with a flat, heavy bottom. This enables you to simmer a sauce for some time with no danger of its sticking or burning. A double saucepan is useful for cooking some of the more temperamental sauces, with hot, not boiling water in the bottom. But if you don't have one a basin put over an ordinary saucepan will serve.

Use a wooden spoon for stirring, but a wire whisk for whisking in egg yolks, cream or butter, also for blending in milk or other liquids. A wooden spatula is useful for getting all of a sauce out of the pan.

Electrical gadgets are not essential, but a food processor is extremely helpful as it chops ingredients neatly (fine, even chopping is very important in sauce-making), mixes efficiently and purées well. A hand-held electric whisk is handy as you can prop it (switched to the lowest speed) on the edge of a small saucepan for sauces that need long, constant stirring. An electric liquidiser makes short work of preparing purées, but a hand-operated food mill will do perfectly well.

CHOOSING A SAUCE TO GO WITH YOUR
FISH DISH

A good sauce can turn a plain dish into something really exciting and requires a relatively short preparation and cooking time giving the dish extra interest and versatility. Plainly cooked fish, especially, tends to cry out for something more than just a quarter of lemon to complement it and even a dish like a mixed fish pie will be transformed from a fairly mundane recipe to a dinner-party special if it is accompanied by a well-flavoured and colourful sauce.

If the fish you are cooking has a special flavouring of its own that needs to be developed rather than overshadowed, then the sauce you serve with it should be gentle rather than aggressive. Freshly grilled bass or grey mullet, for instance, should be partnered with a light white sauce such as parsley, egg or *ravigote* whereas a dish like snippets of fried fish which relies more on its texture than the flavour of the fish itself can happily be married up to one of the more robust sauces such as a spicy home-made tomato or a sauce tartare.

The texture of sauce is also of paramount importance. The base of the sauce must be smooth and it should give an almost satiny sensation to the tongue; chopped ingredients added to the sauce must be *very* finely chopped and not added in great chunks.

Hot Sauces

White Sauce

Dozens of delicious sauces you can serve with plainly cooked fish are based on a white sauce. Make sure the sauce is really smooth and of a good consistency and then add the flavouring ingredients.

> 28 g (1 oz) butter
> 1½ tablespoons flour
> 285 ml (½ pint) milk
> 2 tablespoons single cream
> Salt and pepper

Melt the butter, add the flour and mix well. Gradually blend in the milk, stirring continually over a medium high heat, until the sauce comes to the boil and is thick and smooth. Mix in the cream, season with salt and pepper and simmer, stirring, for 3 minutes.

Variations on White Sauce

Parsley Sauce

285 ml ($\frac{1}{2}$ pint) white sauce
3 tablespoons minced or very finely chopped parsley
1 teaspoon lemon juice

Make the white sauce. Add the parsley and lemon juice – mix well and simmer for 3 minutes before serving.

Serve with a well-flavoured but plainly cooked fish dish such as grilled or baked fillets of coley or with fishcakes.

Egg Sauce

2 hard-boiled eggs
285 ml ($\frac{1}{2}$ pint) white sauce
1 tablespoon double cream
$\frac{1}{2}$ teaspoon made English mustard
Pinch cayenne pepper

Finely chop the hard-boiled eggs. Make the white sauce, add the eggs, cream and mustard and mix well over a low heat without boiling. Season with a pinch of cayenne and serve at once.

Serve with plainly cooked, grilled fish.

Ravigote Sauce

1 tablespoon finely chopped fresh parsley
$\frac{1}{2}$ tablespoon each finely chopped fresh tarragon, cress tops, chervil and sorrel if available
285 ml ($\frac{1}{2}$ pint) white sauce
1 teaspoon lemon juice
4 tablespoons double or single cream
Salt and freshly ground black pepper

Add the herbs to the sauce and beat in the lemon juice. Heat through, add the cream and season with salt and black pepper. Do not boil once the cream has been added.

Serve with grilled, fried or poached fish. Ravigote sauce makes a good accompaniment to grilled mackerel.

Mustard Sauce

This tart, sharp sauce is good with fish of all kinds but especially the more oily ones like mackerel.

> 1 teaspoon made English mustard
> 1 tablespoon white wine vinegar
> 285 ml ($\frac{1}{2}$ pint) white sauce
> 1 tablespoon finely chopped dill leaves (optional)

Mix the mustard and vinegar until smooth. Make the white sauce, add the mustard and vinegar mixture and mix well over a low heat. Add the dill leaves (if used) and stir for 3 minutes before serving.

Serve with fried or grilled fish and especially with fried fillets of perch, grilled mackerel or with deep-fried whitebait.

Prawn Sauce

> 285 ml ($\frac{1}{2}$ pint) white sauce
> 57–113 g (2–4 oz) very finely chopped peeled prawns
> $\frac{1}{2}$ teaspoon lemon juice
> Few drops anchovy essence
> Pinch cayenne pepper

Make the white sauce. Add the prawns, lemon juice, anchovy essence and cayenne and mix well until the ingredients are hot through. Serve at once as the prawns will harden if they are left for any length of time.

A versatile sauce that goes well with any plainly cooked

fish and also makes a sophisticated addition to fishcakes or a fish pie.

Caper Sauce

Another rather sharp sauce that goes well with poached or baked fish.

> 285 ml ($\frac{1}{2}$ pint) white sauce
> 2 tablespoons very finely chopped capers

Make the sauce, add the capers and cook for 3 minutes over a low heat before serving.

Cream Sauce

This is richer version of white sauce: substitute single cream for half the quantity of milk. Make sure it does not boil after the cream has been added.

White Wine Sauce

Use half quantities of milk and half of dry white wine when making the basic white sauce.

Béchamel Sauce

This is the same as a white sauce but the milk has flavourings infused into it before being added to the butter and flour *roux*.

> 1 blade of mace
> 1 bay leaf
> 1 slice onion
> 4 peppercorns
> 285 ml ($\frac{1}{2}$ pint) milk

28 g (1 oz) butter
1½ tablespoons flour
2 tablespoons single cream
Salt and pepper

Combine the mace, bay leaf, onion and peppercorns in a small saucepan with the milk and bring slowly to the boil. Remove the milk as soon as it comes to the boil and strain it through a fine sieve. Leave the milk to cool while making the *roux*.

Melt the butter, add the flour and mix well. Gradually add the milk, stirring continually over a medium heat until the sauce comes to the boil and is thick and smooth. Mix in the cream, simmer for 3 minutes, stirring, and then season with salt and pepper.

Variations on Béchamel Sauce

Sauce Aurore

285 ml (½ pint) béchamel sauce
4 tablespoons very strong home-made tomato sauce
   (see page 222)
2 tablespoons single cream

Make the béchamel sauce as above, add the tomato sauce and mix well. Add the extra cream and check the seasoning before serving.

Serve with almost any poached fish, with Fritto Misto di Mare or with Coley and Prawn Pie.

Mushroom Sauce

85 g (3 oz) firm button mushrooms
14 g (½ oz) butter
Salt and pepper, a pinch of nutmeg and of cayenne
285 ml (½ pint) béchamel sauce
4 tablespoons single cream

Very thinly slice the mushrooms. Heat the butter in a small saucepan. Add the mushrooms and cook over a medium high heat, stirring to prevent sticking, for 3 minutes until the butter has been absorbed (if the mushrooms are really firm and are cooked over a high enough heat they should not give out any extra liquid). Season the mushrooms with salt, pepper, cayenne and nutmeg and mix them well so that they absorb the seasonings. Add the mushrooms to the sauce, mix in the cream and heat through without boiling.

Mornay or Cheese Sauce

This is one of the most classic and delicious of sauces to serve with fish providing it is well made. Do try and use a combination of Gruyère and Parmesan cheese rather than just Cheddar as the flavour really is better, and keep a little of the cheese to sprinkle over the top of the finished dish so that you can put it under a grill and produce a gorgeously bubbling and golden topping.

> 285 ml ($\frac{1}{2}$ pint) béchamel sauce
> 28 g (1 oz) Gruyère cheese, grated
> 14 g ($\frac{1}{2}$ oz) Parmesan cheese, very finely grated
> 4 tablespoons single cream
> Salt, pepper and nutmeg
> 1 teaspoon made English mustard

Make the béchamel sauce, remove it from the heat and beat in the cheese, stirring until it melts. Add the cream, season with salt, pepper and nutmeg and stir in the mustard. Heat the sauce through gently without boiling.

For a quick supper dish, half-grill fillets of white fish such as pollock or coley, top with mornay sauce and return to the grill. Cook until the top of the sauce is golden brown and bubbling.

Velouté Sauce

A white sauce made with fish stock rather than milk which forms the basis of many delicious sauces to serve with fish. If you have no fish stock you can use chicken.

> 57 g (2 oz) butter
> 3½ tablespoons flour
> 570 ml (1 pint) reduced fish stock (see page 67)
> Salt and pepper

Melt the butter, add the flour and mix well over a low heat without browning until the flour and butter form a ball and come away from the sides of the pan. Gradually beat in the stock, stirring continually over a medium high heat, until the sauce comes to the boil and is thick and smooth. Add the seasonings and heat through. For a richer sauce add a few tablespoons double cream.

Variations on Velouté Sauce

Sauce Allemande

> 1 teaspoon lemon juice
> 1 egg yolk
> Basic velouté sauce

Beat the lemon juice with the egg yolk until the mixture is completely smooth. Make the velouté sauce; lower the heat to the lowest possible level and beat in the lemon juice and egg yolk mixture, stirring continually until the sauce is completely smooth and nicely thickened.

Essentially a sauce for a well-flavoured and textured poached or baked fish dish.

Soubise or Onion Sauce

    2 onions
    ½ quantity basic velouté sauce
    142 ml (¼ pint) single cream

Peel and chop the onions. Cover them with cold water and bring to the boil. Strain the onions, cover them with more cold water and boil until the onions are tender.

Drain the onions and rub them through a fine sieve, or put through a food mill or in a liquidiser.

Make the velouté sauce, add the onions and cream and heat through without boiling. Adjust the seasoning before serving.

A good accompaniment to grilled fish cutlets or steaks.

Tomato Velouté

Add 4 tablespoons rich tomato sauce (home-made) and 28 g (1 oz) butter to 570 ml (1 pint) velouté sauce and season with salt and freshly ground black pepper.

Sauce Bercy

This has a delicious flavour but it can swamp the taste of the fish itself, so serve it with the more mildly-flavoured fish like pollock, red fish, fried dabs, etc.

    1 small shallot
    5 tablespoons white wine
    Salt and freshly ground black pepper
    570 ml (1 pint) velouté sauce
    28 g (1 oz) butter
    1 tablespoon mixed finely chopped chives, chervil and
      parsley

Peel and very finely chop the shallot and put it into a small saucepan with the white wine. Season well with salt and pepper, bring to the boil and cook over a high heat until the wine has almost evaporated and the shallot is soft. Add the shallot and juices to the basic velouté sauce, mix in the butter cut into small pieces and stir in the herbs. Check seasoning before serving.

Sauce Poulette

This is a rich version of the basic velouté sauce and very much a sauce for an occasion. Do not boil the sauce once the egg yolks have been added; just heat through (the yolks are used as an enrichment rather than a thickener).

> 1 shallot
> 142 ml (¼ pint) white wine
> 285 ml (½ pint) velouté sauce
> 2 egg yolks
> Salt and freshly ground black pepper
> Juice of 1 lemon
> 1 tablespoon finely chopped parsley
> Pinch grated nutmeg
> 28 g (1 oz) butter

Peel and very finely chop the shallot. Add the wine and cook over a high heat until the liquid is reduced to about 1 tablespoon. Heat the velouté sauce gently, stirring continuously. Beat the egg yolks and beat in 1 tablespoon of the hot sauce. Add to the sauce in the pan with the shallot and its juices, season with salt and pepper and beat in the lemon juice, parsley and a little nutmeg. Heat through, stirring all the time, without boiling and, when the sauce is thoroughly hot and shining, beat in the butter cut into small pieces.

Sauce Allette

> 42 g (1½ oz) butter
> 3 tablespoons flour
> 142 ml (¼ pint) fish or chicken stock
> 2 tablespoons Parmesan cheese
> 1 egg yolk
> 142 ml (¼ pint) single cream
> Salt and cayenne pepper

Melt the butter in a small heavy saucepan. Add the flour and mix well. Gradually blend in the stock, stirring continually over a medium heat until the sauce is thick and smooth. Lower the heat as much as possible and beat in the cheese. Beat the egg yolk with the cream until smooth. Add the egg and cream mixture to the sauce and stir over the low heat until it becomes thick and satiny and the cheese has melted. Season with salt and cayenne pepper.

Drawn Butter Sauce

An old-fashioned sauce that can well do with a bit of publicity. It has a rich buttery flavour and is a good accompaniment for a well-flavoured but plainly cooked fish.

> 113 g (4 oz) butter
> 3 tablespoons flour
> 425 ml (¾ pint) fish stock
> Salt and pepper
> 1 teaspoon lemon juice

Melt half the butter in a small heavy pan. Add the flour and mix well until the flour and butter form a ball and come cleanly away from the sides of the pan. Gradually blend in the stock, stirring continually over a medium high heat until the sauce comes to the boil and is thick and smooth. Season with salt and pepper and blend in the lemon juice. Add the remaining butter cut into small pieces and continue to stir over a medium heat until it has melted and been absorbed into the sauce.

Variations

Add 57 g (2 oz) finely chopped peeled prawns to the finished sauce.

Add 2 tablespoons finely chopped capers to the finished sauce.

Add 2 finely chopped hard-boiled eggs to the sauce with either 1 teaspoon lemon juice or 1 teaspoon made English mustard.

Tomato Sauce

> 1 onion
> 2 cloves garlic
> 1 carrot
> 900 g (2 lb) fresh tomatoes or 1 large tin peeled tomatoes
> 2 tablespoons olive or vegetable oil
> Pinch sugar
> 1 teaspoon white wine vinegar
> 2 bay leaves
> $\frac{1}{2}$ teaspoon dried oregano or fresh basil
> Salt and freshly ground black pepper

Peel and very finely chop the onion. Peel and crush the garlic cloves. Peel and very finely chop or coarsely grate the carrot. Prepare fresh tomatoes by covering them with boiling water for 1 minute. Drain off the water and slide off the skins. Heat the oil in a heavy saucepan. Add the onion and garlic and cook over a low heat, stirring every now and then, until they become transparent and soft. Add the carrot, tomatoes, sugar, vinegar, bay leaves and herbs, season with salt and pepper, bring to the boil and cook over a medium heat until the sauce is reduced to a thick stew consistency and the tomatoes are well broken up. Stir every now and then to prevent sticking. Remove the bay leaves and serve the sauce as it is, or sieve to remove the pips.

The tomato and Espagnole sauce variations have an extremely robust flavour and can lift the plainest dishes to unexpected heights. Try serving with a fish pie, with fish-cakes or with a dish like Pilaf with Monk Fish or Huss and Ham (see page 120).

Variations on Tomato Sauce

Make a more spicy sauce by adding 2 finely chopped, cored and seeded red peppers and a very, very finely chopped chilli pepper.

Flavour with a little thyme as well as some finely chopped fresh basil leaves.

Add 2 tablespoons of white wine instead of the vinegar.

Add the finely grated rind and juice of half an orange.

Make a thick tomato purée by boiling the sauce without a lid until thick and reduced to about a third. Rub the purée through a sieve or a fine food mill.

Creamy Tomato Sauce

This is a useful sauce which takes little time to make and can be used to stretch a small amount of fish. Make the sauce and add to it some cooked flaked or cubed fish or some peeled cooked prawns or other shellfish. Heat through and serve in a ring of boiled rice.

 1 225-g (8-oz) tin tomatoes
 1 stalk celery
 Sprig thyme
 Small bay leaf
 Salt and cayenne pepper
 57 g (2 oz) butter
 2 tablespoons flour

285 ml ($\frac{1}{2}$ pint) milk
Salt and freshly ground black pepper

Roughly chop up the tomatoes and finely chop the celery.
Combine them with the thyme and bay leaf in a saucepan,
season with salt and cayenne pepper, bring to the boil and
simmer for 20 minutes. Pass the sauce through a fine sieve
or food mill.

Melt the butter, add the flour and mix well until the
butter and flour form a ball and come cleanly away from the
sides of the pan. Gradually blend in the milk, stirring
continually over a medium heat until the sauce comes to the
boil and is thick and smooth. Add the strained tomato
mixture, mix well, simmer for 3 minutes and check the
seasoning before serving.

Espagnole Sauce for Fish

Tomatoes and fish go extremely well together, and this
version of a classic sauce is delicious with plainly cooked
fish of almost any kind.

1 shallot or small onion
1 carrot
4 small button mushrooms
57 g (2 oz) butter
57 g (2 oz) flour
570 ml (1 pint) brown stock
2 large tomatoes
Salt and freshly ground black pepper

Peel and very finely chop the onion or shallot. Peel and
coarsely grate the carrot. Very finely chop the mushrooms.
Melt the butter, add the onion or shallot, the carrot and the
mushrooms and cook over a medium heat until the onion is
golden brown. Add the flour and stir over a medium high
heat until the flour has turned nut brown. Gradually add
the stock, stirring until the sauce comes to the boil and is
thick and smooth.

Roughly chop the tomatoes and add them to the sauce. Season with salt and pepper, cover and simmer for 10 minutes. Strain the sauce through a fine sieve or pass it through a fine food mill.

Variations on Espagnole Sauce

Piquante Sauce

>   2 teaspoons capers
>   1 shallot or small onion
>   1 gherkin
>   2 tablespoons red wine vinegar
>   1 teaspoon finely chopped parsley
> $\frac{1}{2}$ quantity of Espagnole sauce

Very finely chop the capers, shallot or onion, and gherkin. Combine the vinegar, shallot, capers, gherkin and parsley in a saucepan, bring to the boil and cook over a high heat until the vinegar has been absorbed. Add this mixture to the Espagnole sauce and heat through.

Italienne Sauce

> $\frac{1}{2}$ quantity Espagnole sauce (unsieved)
>   1 bouquet garni
>   2 tablespoons medium dry sherry
>   Salt and freshly ground black pepper

Make the Espagnole sauce (as above). Add the bouquet garni and sherry, season with a little additional salt and pepper, bring to the boil and simmer gently for 15 minutes. Remove the bouquet garni. Strain the sauce through a fine sieve or pass through a fine food mill.

Mousseline Sauce

A superior sauce, this is light but rich.

2 egg yolks
2 teaspoons lemon juice
42 g (1½ oz) butter
3 tablespoons flour
285 ml (½ pint) fish or chicken stock
Salt and pepper
142 ml (¼ pint) single or double cream

Beat the egg yolks with the lemon juice until smooth. Melt the butter in a small, heavy saucepan. Add the flour and mix well until the flour and butter form a ball and come cleanly away from the sides of the pan. Gradually blend in the stock, stirring continually over a medium high heat until the sauce comes to the boil and is thick and smooth. Season with salt and pepper and simmer for 3 minutes. Lower the heat until the sauce is below simmering point and beat in the cream, egg yolks and lemon juice.

The sauce should be served as quickly as possible after it has been made. Makes a delicious accompaniment to the Gigot of Monk Fish (see page 157).

Sauce Angélique

A slightly crunchy sauce with a somewhat sharp flavour.

57 g (2 oz) shredded almonds
8 stuffed olives
42 g (1½ oz) butter
3 tablespoons flour
285 ml (½ pint) chicken stock
Salt and a little cayenne pepper
142 ml (¼ pint) single cream
2 teaspoons lemon juice

Roast the almonds in a hot oven for about 3 minutes until they are crisp and very lightly browned. Cut the olives into thin slices.

Melt the butter in a small saucepan. Add the flour and mix well until the flour and butter form a ball and come smoothly away from the sides of the pan. Gradually beat in the stock, stirring continually over a medium high heat until the sauce comes to the boil and is thick and smooth. Simmer for 3 minutes and season with a little salt and cayenne pepper. Lower the heat to below simmering point and mix in the cream, almonds, olives and lemon juice.

Good with the plainer fish dishes or with sprats, white-bait, crabs or fried fillets of fish.

Cider Sauce

> 285 ml ($\frac{1}{2}$ pint) cider
> 42 g ($1\frac{1}{2}$ oz) butter
> 4 tablespoons flour
> 425 ml ($\frac{3}{4}$ pint) fish stock (see page 67)
> Salt and freshly ground pepper

Put the cider into a small saucepan, bring to the boil and cook over a fast heat until reduced by half. Melt the butter in a small saucepan. Add the flour and mix well until the butter and flour form a ball and come cleanly away from the sides of the pan. Gradually beat in the stock, stirring continually over a medium high heat until the sauce comes to the boil and is thick and smooth. Add the cider, season with salt and pepper and simmer for 3 minutes.

Fennel Sauce

Although traditionally used as an accompaniment to mackerel I have successfully combined this interesting celery/aniseed flavour with a great many other plainly cooked fish dishes. Florence fennel can be bought from better greengrocers' towards the end of the summer and can also easily be grown in the garden.

    1 fennel bulb
    1 small onion
    57 g (2 oz) butter
    2 tablespoons flour
    285 ml ($\frac{1}{2}$ pint) fish or chicken stock
    Salt and pepper
    1 egg yolk
    142 ml ($\frac{1}{4}$ pint) double cream
    142 ml ($\frac{1}{4}$ pint) dry white wine

Trim off the top and bottom of the fennel bulb and remove any tough outer leaves. Very finely shred the root. Peel and finely chop the onion.

Melt the butter in a small, heavy saucepan. Add the onion and fennel and cook over a low heat, stirring every now and then until the onion is transparent and the fennel soft. Sprinkle over the flour and mix well. Gradually blend in the stock, stirring continually over a medium high heat until the sauce comes to the boil and is thick and smooth. Season with salt and pepper and simmer slowly for 5 minutes.

Beat the egg yolk with the cream and white wine until the mixture is absolutely smooth. Lower the heat to below simmering and beat in the cream mixture, stirring all the time until the sauce thickens and has a glossy sheen.

Asparagus Sauce

Make this with tinned asparagus pieces; far cheaper than whole asparagus.

    1 small tin asparagus pieces
    Milk
    57 g (2 oz) butter
    3 tablespoons flour

142 ml (¼ pint) chicken stock
1 teaspoon lemon juice
Salt and pepper
1 egg yolk (optional)

Drain off the liquid from the asparagus and add enough milk to make up 285 ml (½ pint) of liquid. Melt the butter in a small, heavy saucepan. Add the flour and mix well. Gradually blend in the asparagus/milk and chicken stock, stirring continually over a medium high heat until the sauce comes to the boil and is thick and smooth. Blend in the lemon juice and season with salt and pepper. Add the asparagus pieces and simmer gently for 3 minutes.

For a richer sauce beat an egg yolk into the white sauce before the asparagus is added. Do not allow the sauce to boil after this.

A good sauce to serve with grilled red mullet, grilled mackerel or with baked fish steaks.

Devil Paste

This was traditionally a paste rubbed into meat before grilling, but I found that it is also extremely good rubbed into cutlets or steaks of white fish or fillets of mackerel. I can highly recommend this process for steaks of frozen fish which might otherwise be uninteresting.

1 teaspoon French Dijon mustard
1 teaspoon made English mustard
57 g (2 oz) butter
1 teaspoon lemon juice
Salt, pepper and a pinch cayenne

Combine all the ingredients and work to a smooth paste. Score the fish with a sharp knife through the skin or just below the surface of the flesh and rub the paste into the flesh before grilling.

Beurre Noire

The classic sauce to serve with skate wings, this is also good
with any very fresh and tender grilled fish. Put 57 g (2 oz)
butter, preferably unsalted, in a small frying pan and cook
it over a high flame until it turns the colour of ripe hazelnuts.
Remove from the heat immediately before it darkens any
further – although it is called black butter is must only be
allowed to brown.

Cardinal Sauce

This should really be made from lobster coral but since the
price of lobster is so prohibitive I have been trying to make
the sauce with alternative ingredients and have come up
with some very good substitutes. It is a rich sauce and goes
well with some of the rather more plain poached-fish dishes
or with the Savoury Fish Creams on page 166.

>   57 g (2 oz) prawns or brown crab meat
>   57 g (2 oz) butter
>   21 g ($\frac{3}{4}$ oz) flour
>   285 ml ($\frac{1}{2}$ pint) fish stock (see page 67)
>   Juice of $\frac{1}{2}$ small lemon
>   70 ml ($2\frac{1}{2}$ fl oz) cream
>   Salt, freshly ground black pepper and nutmeg

Pound the prawns or crab meat to a smooth paste with half
the butter. Melt the remaining butter in a saucepan, add
the flour and mix well. Gradually blend in the stock,
stirring continually over a medium high heat until the sauce
comes to the boil and is thick and smooth. Add the lemon
juice, flavoured butter and cream, season with salt, pepper
and a pinch of nutmeg and heat through *without boiling*.

SAUCES WITH ADDED FISH

These sauces are ideal for using with a fish dish that might otherwise be rather mundane, or for giving a luxury taste to an inexpensive fish.

Potted Shrimp Sauce

Although this is rather expensive it is so quick to make, and so delicious, that you can use it to dress up even the cheapest of fish.

> 1 small carton potted shrimps
> 57 g (2 oz) butter
> $\frac{1}{2}$ teaspoon lemon juice
> Freshly ground black pepper and a pinch of cayenne
> 2 tablespoons double cream

Put the shrimps into a saucepan with the butter and cook over a low heat until all the butter has melted and the shrimps are hot through. Add the lemon juice and season with pepper and cayenne. Blend in the cream and heat through without boiling.

Anchovy Sauce

The salty taste of anchovy provides one of the best partners to other fish dishes.

> 4 anchovy fillets
> 113 g (4 oz) butter
> Cayenne pepper and a pinch of mace

Pound the anchovy fillets to a smooth paste in a mortar. Melt the butter in a small heavy saucepan. Add the anchovy paste and mix well. Season with cayenne pepper and a little mace and heat gently for 3 minutes.

Cockle Sauce

In moments of extreme belt tightening this simple little sauce can well stand on its own with a dish of pasta. If no fish stock is available use chicken.

> 57 g (2 oz) butter
> 4 tablespoons flour
> 570 ml (1 pint) fish stock (see page 67)
> 170 g (6 oz) fresh or frozen cockles
> Juice of $\frac{1}{2}$ lemon
> Salt and freshly ground black pepper
> 1 tablespoon finely chopped parsley
> 2 teaspoons finely chopped chives or spring onion tops

Melt the butter in a saucepan; add the flour and mix well. Gradually add the stock, stirring over a medium high heat until the sauce comes to the boil and is thick and smooth. Add the cockles and lemon juice, season with salt and pepper, mix in the parsley and chives and heat through without boiling.

FRUIT SAUCES

Because of their sharp, fresh taste, fruit sauces are excellent with fish. Gooseberry sauce is traditional with mackerel, but goes just as well with other fish dishes, hot or cold; plum sauce makes an delicious sweet/sour accompaniment to any grilled or fried fish; curried apple sauce is good with a bland fish, such as coley.

Gooseberry Sauce

> 340 g (12 oz) sharp green gooseberries
> Finely grated rind and the juice of 1 small lemon
> 14 g ($\frac{1}{2}$ oz) butter
> 1 teaspoon castor sugar
> Pinch ground ginger

Place the gooseberries in a saucepan and barely cover them with cold water. Bring to the boil and simmer until soft; pass through a fine sieve or food mill. Place the gooseberry purée in a small saucepan, add the remaining ingredients and heat gently until the butter has melted.

Curried Apple Sauce

 1 cooking apple
 1 shallot or small onion
 28 g (1 oz) butter
 14 g ($\frac{1}{2}$ oz) flour
 14 g ($\frac{1}{2}$ oz) curry powder
 285 ml ($\frac{1}{2}$ pint) chicken or fish stock
 1 teaspoon lemon juice
 Salt and freshly ground black pepper
 Pinch sugar
 2 teaspoons finely chopped chutney

Peel and grate the apple and shallot or small onion. Melt the butter, add the shallot and apple and cook over a low heat until golden brown. Add the flour and curry powder and cook over a moderately high heat, stirring every now and then, until the mixture is a rich golden brown. Add the stock, a little at a time, stirring continually, until the sauce comes to the boil and is thick and smooth. Skim off any fat that rises to the surface of the sauce, strain it through a fine sieve (or put through a liquidiser or food processor) return it to a clean pan and add the lemon juice. Season with salt, pepper and a pinch of sugar, add the chutney and thin, if necessary, with a little extra stock or water – the sauce should be thickish but not cloying.

Plum Sauce

Plum sauces figure largely in Chinese cookery, but considering the amount of plums that are grown for cooking in

Great Britain it is surprising they have never achieved any great merit here.

> 225 g (8 oz) cooking plums
> 285 ml ($\frac{1}{2}$ pint) water
> 1 clove garlic
> Pinch ground coriander
> 1 teaspoon finely chopped fresh basil or a pinch of dried basil
> Salt and cayenne pepper
> 28 g (1 oz) butter

Combine the plums and water in a saucepan, bring to the boil, cover and simmer until the plums are soft (about 20 minutes). Cool, remove the plum stones and purée the plums with the garlic clove in a food mill, liquidiser or food processor.

Return the purée to a clean pan. Add the coriander and basil, season with salt and cayenne pepper and beat in the butter. Bring to the boil, remove from the heat and serve hot or cold.

Hollandaise Sauce

Don't quail at the thought of making this highly sophisticated sauce. The chance that it may separate makes one nervous, but avoiding this only takes time and patience. Don't try and make the sauce in a hurry, don't ever let it boil and be resigned to its taking as long as half an hour to prepare.

> 3 tablespoons white wine vinegar
> 2 tablespoons water
> 8 white peppercorns
> 3 large egg yolks
> 170 g (6 oz) butter
> 2 teaspoons lemon juice
> Salt

Put the vinegar, water and peppercorns into a small saucepan, bring to the boil and cook over a high heat until the
liquid is reduced to about 1 tablespoon. Strain the liquid
and leave to cool. Beat the egg yolks until smooth. Melt
the butter without boiling it. Combine the egg yolks and
vinegar mixture in a basin and stand over a pan of hot, not
boiling, water. Over a low heat, keeping the water in the pan
below boiling point at all times, beat the yolks with a wire
whisk, gradually adding the butter, a little at a time, until the
sauce thickens and is the consistency of mayonnaise. When
the sauce is thick and shining and all the butter has been
absorbed, beat in the lemon juice and season with a little
salt.

The sauce can be covered and left in the bowl, still over
warm water, for some time before it is served.

Béarnaise Sauce

This is made in the same way as Hollandaise sauce but
additional flavour is given by adding herbs and tarragon
vinegar.

    1 tablespoon finely chopped shallot
    1 tablespoon finely chopped fresh tarragon leaves
    1 tablespoon finely chopped fresh chervil leaves
    4 tablespoons white wine
    4 tablespoons tarragon vinegar
    6 white peppercorns
    3 egg yolks
    170 g (6 oz) butter
    Salt and cayenne

Combine the shallot, tarragon, chervil, white wine and
vinegar in a saucepan with the peppercorns. Bring to the
boil and cook over a high heat until the liquid is reduced to
about 2 tablespoons. Strain off the liquid and leave to cool.

Proceed as for Hollandaise, above, and season with salt
and cayenne.

Cold Sauces

Although cold sauces usually accompany cold fish, there are exceptions, such as the classic tartare sauce, traditional with deep-fried fish, and the savoury butters, served chilled but intended to melt temptingly over a hot fish. Most of the cold sauces are based on mayonnaise, so it's well worth mastering the art of making your own.

MAYONNAISE

Of all the classic cold sauces used to accompany cold shell-fish and other fish the best known of all is, of course, mayonnaise, of which there are far too many variations to include in this book. Having completed your rich, smooth, thick and pale mayonnaise you have a foundation which just cries out for the addition of any number of exciting additives. I can only give you the basic sauce and some ideas of the kind of things you can do with it – after that it's up to you.

The secret of this famous sauce lies in the very gradual addition of oil to egg yolks, and in the beating between each addition which results in a rich emulsion. With practice the making of the sauce speeds up, but, if you are new at the game, be prepared to take time over it for if too much oil is added at a time, or if the ingredients are not thoroughly beaten, the sauce will separate. If this happens don't despair; beat in a few drops of vinegar. If this doesn't work start again by beating a third egg yolk and gradually blending and beating the curdled mixture into that, very slowly, making sure that each addition emulsifies before adding more.

Mayonnaise can also be made successfully in a food processor, a liquidiser or with an electric beater, but again the speed at which you add the oil is of paramount importance.

Have all the ingredients at the same temperature and

cool, not chilled or warm; this reduces the risk of separation.

Use standard eggs at least 3 days old.

Olive oil is traditional, but since this has become so very expensive I use sunflower oil as I find this the best compromise between cost and flavour. Good-quality sunflower oil has virtually no flavour, is pale in colour (therefore producing a pale mayonnaise) and its light consistency produces a sauce that is not too heavy and cloying. Avoid stronger-tasting oils like corn and groundnut unless highly refined.

Season your mayonnaise with white pepper rather than the coarsely ground black variety and use white wine vinegar or fresh lemon juice rather than a harsh malt vinegar or a stronger tasting red wine vinegar.

Basic Mayonnaise

Makes 285 ml ($\frac{1}{2}$ pint)

285 ml ($\frac{1}{2}$ pint) olive oil or sunflower oil
2 egg yolks
Pinch dry mustard
Salt and white pepper
2 tablespoons white wine vinegar
1 tablespoon boiling water

Put the oil into a jug with a good pouring lip. Place the egg yolks in a basin and steady the basin by placing it on a damp cloth spread on the working surface. Add the mustard, salt and pepper to the yolks and beat them with a wooden spoon until they are smooth, slightly thickened and becoming paler in colour.

Add a few drops of olive oil and beat it into the egg yolk mixture with your wooden spoon, until it has completely disappeared. Continue to add the oil, still only a few drops at a time and beating well between each addition, until about half the quantity of oil has been used up. By this time the mixture should have emulsified and be thick and stiff. At this point the oil can be added more quickly, in a very thin steady stream, beating all the time. When all the oil has been absorbed, beat in the vinegar as slowly as you did the oil. Check the seasoning and finally beat in a tablespoon of boiling water to balance the sauce. If the sauce is to be kept for some time cover it with a layer of cling film and keep it in a cool place. Or place in a screw-topped jar, where it will keep for up to a week in the bottom of the refrigerator. Do not freeze. Mayonnaise tends to discolour in sunshine so for an outdoor party bring out your mayonnaise or mayonnaise dishes at the last minute.

Variations on Mayonnaise

All the following sauces can be served with cold shellfish (lobster, prawns, crab, scampi, shrimps) and with cold fish of all kinds. I often serve a choice of mayonnaise with cold shellfish or fish dishes; they look attractive and taste delicious.

Mayonnaise with sour cream

For a less rich sauce with an extremely delicate flavour use only three-quarters of the quantity of oil and finish off the sauce by beating in 4 tablespoons of sour cream.

Rose Mayonnaise

Add 3 tablespoons drained and very finely chopped tinned pimento to the finished mayonnaise. Or use a finely chopped red pepper.

Quick Curry Mayonnaise

Use lemon juice instead of vinegar; combine it with 1 teaspoon of curry powder or paste in a small saucepan and heat over a low flame, stirring continually, for 3 minutes. Leave to cool before adding to the mayonnaise base.

Onion and Chive Mayonnaise

Add 1 teaspoon finely grated raw onion and 2 tablespoons finely chopped chives to the finished mayonnaise.

Garlic Mayonnaise

Peel 2–3 cloves garlic and squeeze them through a garlic press. Beat the crushed garlic with the egg yolks before adding the oil.

Green Pepper Mayonnaise

Green peppercorns can be bought in tins and make a very pleasant and unusual flavouring. Pound 2 teaspoons drained green peppercorns to a paste in a mortar and add to the finished mayonnaise.

Sauce Tartare

Add 2 tablespoons very finely chopped capers, 1 teaspoon very finely chopped pickled cucumber or gherkins, 2 teaspoons very finely chopped spring onion tops or chives and 1 teaspoon Dijon mustard to the finished mayonnaise and mix well.

Sweet Pickle Mayonnaise

Add interest to a plain mayonnaise by mixing in some finely chopped sweet pickles or chutney.

Anchovy Mayonnaise

A stronger-tasting mayonnaise that goes well with shellfish or fish that does not have too pronounced a flavour. Pound 2 drained anchovy fillets to a smooth paste in a mortar. Do not add salt to your mayonnaise base and beat in the anchovy paste when it has been completed.

Coating Mayonnaise

Sometimes it is pleasant to coat a cold fish dish with mayonnaise and garnish it prettily to make an attractive centrepiece to a summer meal.

To make a coating of mayonnaise thick enough to remain in place on the fish combine 142 ml ($\frac{1}{4}$ pint) mayonnaise with 142 ml ($\frac{1}{4}$ pint) double cream and mix well. Sprinkle 1 teaspoon powdered gelatine into $1\frac{1}{2}$ tablespoons cold water and mix well. Leave to stand for 5 minutes and then stir in 1 tablespoon boiling water, mixing until the gelatine has completely dissolved.

Blend this mixture into the mayonnaise and cream and leave until the sauce is just beginning to set. Spread the mayonnaise over the fish garnishing them as you do so with slices of stuffed olives, leaves of chervil, small slivers of pickled walnut or strips of pimento.

Mayonnaise as a dressing

I you are using mayonnaise as a dressing for a salad thin it down by beating in some double or single cream, or sour cream.

Other flavourings for mayonnaise

Instead of ordinary salt, use celery or garlic salt, or one of the seasoning salts now on sale.

Replace the pepper with a little cayenne or paprika.

Any finely chopped fresh herbs can be added to a mayonnaise – try a combination of very finely chopped parsley, chervil and chives.

Add a few finely chopped peeled prawns.

Peel and grate half a cucumber and leave to drain in a sieve for 30 minutes before patting it dry and adding to the mayonnaise base; or use a dill pickled cucumber.

Add some finely grated raw horseradish or a spoonful of horseradish sauce to give a pleasantly sharp flavour.

Avranches Sauce

This is a delicious summer sauce that gives a dream-like quality to salmon or cold trout if one can afford it, and also lifts less budget-breaking fish into the class of *haute cuisine*.

285 ml (½ pint) double cream
1 tablespoon very, very finely chopped parsley
1 tablespoon minced shallot
1 tablespoon finely chopped chervil or chives
1 tablespoon tomato purée
Salt and freshly ground black pepper
1 tablespoon finely chopped capers
1 teaspoon lemon juice
28 g (1 oz) butter

Put the cream into a small heavy saucepan and heat it to below boiling point (do not allow to boil on any account). Add the herbs and whisk in the tomato purée with a small wire whisk. Season with salt and pepper and mix in the capers, shallot and lemon juice. Cook very gently for a few minutes and stir in the butter just before serving.

Orange, Dubonnet and Horseradish Sauce

This unusual sauce is a perfect accompaniment either to cold smoked mackerel or hot fried fillets of mackerel or other fish.

142 ml (¼ pint) double cream
1 tablespoon made horseradish sauce
Grated rind and juice of 1 orange
2 tablespoons Dubonnet
Salt and pepper

Whip the cream until thick. Add the horseradish sauce and gradually blend in the orange juice and Dubonnet, beating all the time so that the sauce remains thick. Add the orange rind, season with salt and pepper, pile in a bowl and serve well chilled.

Cucumber Sauce

This is a perfect foil to fried or grilled fish, particularly in
hot weather.

2 small or 1 large cucumbers
Salt and white pepper
1½ tablespoons white wine vinegar
142 ml (¼ pint) double cream

Peel the cucumber and cut into very small dice, or grate
through a coarse grater. Sprinkle with a little salt and leave
to drain in a sieve for 30 minutes. Whip the cream until
thick. Add the cucumber, season with pepper and gradually
blend in the vinegar.

SAVOURY BUTTERS

With fried, grilled or poached fish instead of serving a
sauce, serve a chilled savoury butter.

As the butter will keep for some time in a refrigerato and
can also be used as a topping for grilled or fried meat,
hamburgers, etc., it is worth making double the basic
quantity at a time. Butters can also be frozen.

Many of the butters can be made in a liquidiser or food
processor.

Parsley or Maître d'Hôtel Butter

This is the classic savoury butter; all the others are made in
the same way.

113 g (4 oz) softened butter
2 tablespoons very finely chopped parsley
½ teaspoon lemon juice
Salt and pepper

Beat the butter until creamy and mix in the chopped

parsley, lemon juice and seasoning. Form into a sausage shape about 25 mm (1 in) in diameter, wrap firmly in foil and chill in the refrigerator until very firm. To use, cut the chilled butter into thin slices.

Chive Butter

Substitute 2 tablespoons of finely chopped chives for the parsley used above.

Garlic Butter

Crush 2 cloves garlic and add them to the softened butter with a good screw of freshly ground black pepper.

Prawn Butter

Mince or pound 113 g (4 oz) prawns to a paste and mix this into the softened butter with a seasoning of a little cayenne pepper.

Anchovy Butter

This is also delicious spread on hot toast, or a square of bread with the crusts removed, baked in a hot oven until crisp. Pound 4–6 drained fillets of anchovy to a smooth paste and mix into the softened butter.

Orange Butter

The sharper the oranges the better the result will be; Seville oranges (available January–February) are ideal. Mix 2 teaspoons orange juice and 1 tablespoon finely grated orange peel into the softened butter.

Tomato Butter

Mix 2 tablespoon tomato purée into the softened butter.

Herb Butter

Blanch the tops of some parsley stalks, some tarragon leaves and some chervil in boiling water for 1 minute and drain really well. Finely chop the herbs and mix them into the softened butter with a little lemon juice to bring out their flavour.

Smoked Salmon Butter

A luxury, but one that can be made with less expensive smoked salmon trimmings, and which adds a delicious flavour to inexpensive fish dishes.

Mince or pound 113 g (4 oz) smoked salmon to a paste. Mix into softened butter with a few drops of lemon juice and a pinch of cayenne pepper.

Curried Butter

Add 1 teaspoon curry powder to the softened butter with $\frac{1}{2}$ teaspoon of lemon juice.

Mustard Butter

Mix 1 teaspoon Dijon mustard into the softened butter and season with salt and freshly ground black pepper. For a sharper butter use made English mustard.

Devilled Butter

Beat 2 teaspoons Dijon mustard and a few drops of Worcestershire and Tabasco sauce into the softened butter.

Some Non-British Equivalent or Substitute Fish

BRITISH NAMES	US NAMES	AUSTRALIAN NAMES	NEW ZEALAND NAMES
*Bass	Bass, Sea Bass, Sea Perch, White Sea Perch		Blue Cod
Brill (*Scophthalmus rhombus*)	Brill		Brill, Turbot
Clams	Clam, Soft Shell Clam, Hard Shell Clam, Surf Clam		
Coley/Saithe (*Pollachius virens*)	Pollock	Rock Cod	Ling
Conger Eel (*Conger conger*)	Conger Eel		Conger
Crab	Crab, Blue Crab, King Crab, Stone Crab, Snow Crab		Crab (very small)
Dabs (*Limanda limanda*)	Dab, Common Dab, Sand Dab, Dab Sole	Flounder	Sand Flounder, Flounder

BRITISH NAMES	US NAMES	AUSTRALIAN NAMES	NEW ZEALAND NAMES
Gurnet or Gurnard	Gurnard, Grey/Red Gurnard, Sea Robin	Red Gurnard, Latchet	Gurnard, Red Gurnard
Huss (*Squalidae*)	Dogfish, Spiny Dogfish	Dog Shark	Spiny/Piked Dogfish
John Dory (*Zeidae, Zenopsis ocellata*)	John Dory, American John Dory	John Dory	John Dory
Mackerel (*Scomber scombrus*)	Mackerel	School or Spanish Mackerel	Blue/Southern Mackerel
Megrim (*Lepidorhombus whiff-iagonis*)	Megrim	Flounder	Sand Flounder
Monk Fish (*Lophius spp*)	Anglerfish, Angler, Angel Shark		Monk Fish
Mullet, Grey (*Mugil ramada*)	Mullet, Grey/Silver Mullet	Sea Mullet	Grey Mullet
Mullet, Red (*Mullet surmuletus*)	Surmullet, Red Mullet		Red Mullet
Perch	Red Fish, Ocean Perch	English Perch	

Pollock (*Pollachius virens*)	Pollock, Pollack, Alaska Pollock	Rock Cod	Ling
Queens (*Chlamys opercularis*)	Scallop		Scallop, Fan Escallop
*Red Fish (*Sebastes spp*)	Red Fish, Ocean Perch	Red Fish	Snapper
Roach	Roach	English Perch	
*Sea Bream (*Sparidae*)	Bream, Sea Bream, Pinfish	Trevally,	Snapper
Skate	Skate, Ray	Skate	Skate
Sprats (*Sprattus sprattus*)	Sprat	Small Pilchards	Sprats
Squid/Cuttlefish (*Loligo vulgaris*)	Squid, Common Squid		Squid
*Whitebait (young of herring or sprat)	Silverside	Even Smaller Pilchards	
*Whiting (*Merlangius merlangus*)	Whiting	School or Goldenlined Whiting	

* These names are sometimes applied to various New Zealand fish which are by no means the same from the culinary point of view.

Index

Grey Mullet
Whiting
John Dory
Red fish
Sea bream
Pollock
Horse Mackerel
Crab
Brill
Megrim Sole.
Gurnard
Queen Shell
Macke